Kris Hagan

The Penis On The Table

The first English book that teaches you there's more than one way of using your tongue.

INTERNATIONAL LANGUAGE INSTITUTE

Who is Kris Hagan?

Born in Manchester (UK), Kris Hagan is the founder and director of his language institute, which teaches over 10 languages. After moving to Italy in 2009, he became the English coach of several esteemed professionals in the medicine, university and communication fields. He has coached internationally-known singers, actors, radio presenters and journalists. Alongside his activities as a teacher, he is also the creator of the free online English magazine Sir.K, the host of the English Uncovered podcast and you can also find him in numerous videos on our YouTube channel.

Kris Hagan - The Penis On The Table

This innovative sExercise book is for all those people out there who keep slipping up when it cums to speaking English during your intimate moments. Or when you are trying to tell someone you want to eat out with your mother and end up saying you want to eat your mother out (true story)!

The penis on the table is only meant for educational needs and no STDs will be transferred. I wrote what you have in your hands right now for all those people out there who are too scared to ask their teacher "How do I ask for a blow job?" or "What's the meaning of cunt?"
Now there is a teacher out there who is willing to break down the embarrassment barrier (bareback)! Me.

This colouring book is not meant to be offensive. We have included many different couples in our amazing illustrations by @dickof_theday, who didn't only draw dicks but gave us a wide range of fun colouring opportunities.

The perfect gift for anyone with a sex drive!

Dedicated to Giorgio Laini, Enrico Pasqualin, Giorgia (who I don't understand) Maniglio, Trees are Green, Mr Poo, The Fairy Duo (who surprisingly aren't a gay couple!), Antonio and Grace, Aristoteles Nici aka Joel, Robusto, Phantom, Geremia and Barberino.

Extra special dedications go to mum (who did the exercises to check they work and was a very proud mother), dad (who did nothing but pass his dirty mind down to me) and any other family members I actually speak to. My wee brother is too young for this book but on his 18th I will be sure to give him a copy.

INDEX

INTRODUCTION

What a difference a space makes…

Who would have thought that during your first lesson of English you misunderstood what the teacher wrote up on the board.

Yes, we know how to order a steak in a restaurant, buy a ticket for the next train to Edinburgh or have small talk at the office but what about the topic we all talk about on a daily basis.
(Or is that just me?)

As we all love talking about this topic I decided to create this book to bring us all together.

So let's join hands (wash them first!) and have a laugh completing this
English sExercise Book.

CHALLENGE 1

Before we get started into the juicy, tasty section of this book we need to be sure we know what we are talking about. Don't you agree?
Let's start off with the first exercise.

What's that?

Label the parts of these beautifully illustrated reproductive organs.
Let's start with a penis.

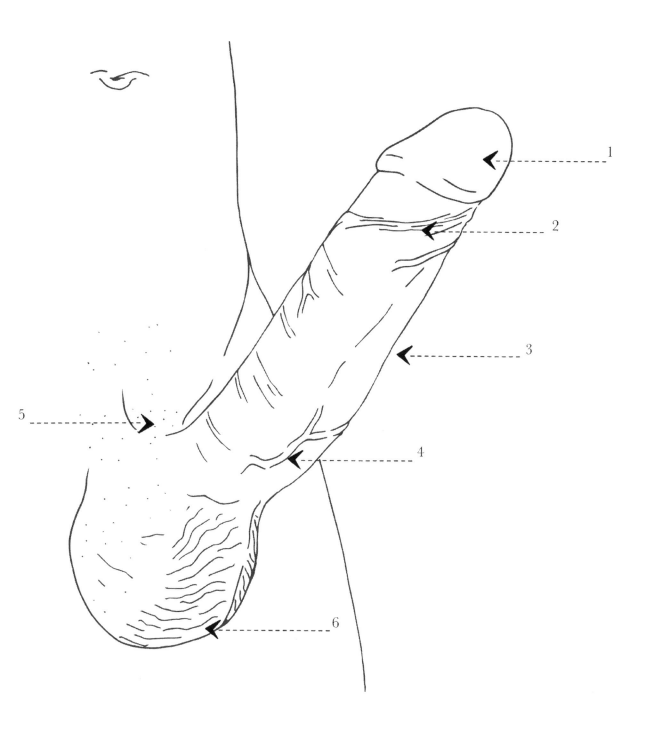

1

2

3

4

5

6

CHALLENGE 2

And now the scientific part. See what you remember from school.

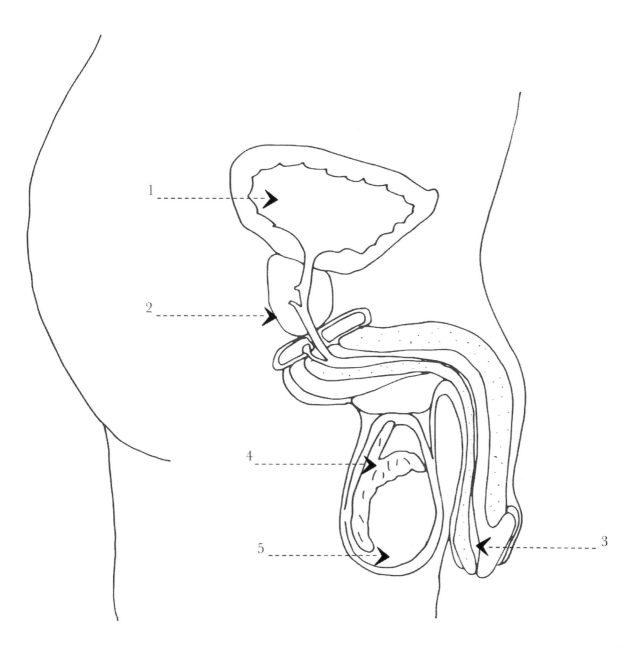

CHALLENGE 3

Here comes the vagina. See if you are one of those who don't know where the clit is.

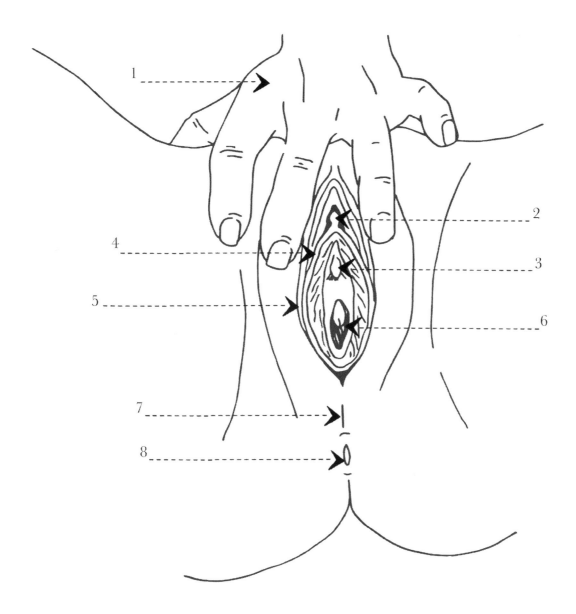

1
2
4
3
5
6
7
8

CHALLENGE 4

And now where we all came from.

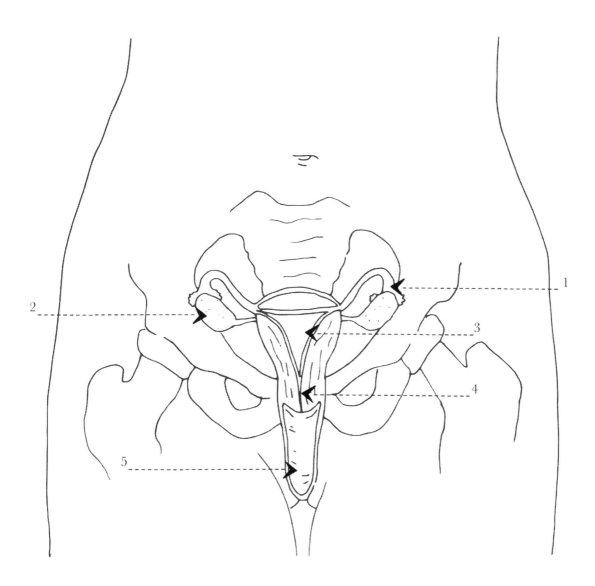

So, now that you have proven you know your way around a penis and a vagina let's go deeper.

THE COCK

The thing which we sometimes call a penis (unless you are a doctor) has many names. Below is a list of just some of the many. They have been jumbled up. Can you correct them? There are some clues by the side of each one.

dcik (Short for Richard. Not his penis, his name.)

_____

icprk (You can do this with a needle. Not really a compliment then.)

_____

mberme (Of parliament? Well…)

_____

ootl (I do love a bit of D.I.Y.)

_____

nokb (You put your hands on these more than you know.)

_____

mleypao (Men love dancing around one of these in the UK.)

_____

ndog (Ding…)

_____

lewnki (Also a small sea snail. Another non-flattering name.)

_____

liylw (What babies call their penis.)

_____

jstiocky (I am sure you played with one of these on a daily basis if you were born in the 80s.)

_____

eownap (Stand back I have a …)

_____

koepct eocrkt (When it is standing to attention it looks like a …)

_____

pcrkee (Woody Wood…)

_____

dgaret (Sounds like a cute black and white animal.)

_____

sngloch (A word that makes it sound longer than it probably is.)

_____

idwieg (Apparently a young woman back in the 50s who has a specific style was called one of these.)

_____

team (Not for veggies)

_____

vole mlescu (How romantic, but you still won't get me to go to a gym.)

_____

wcki (Again I wouldn't use this. It isn't much of a compliment.)

_____

lveo cikst (I wouldn't put wood inside an orifice but it sounds nicer with the first part.)

_____

strdacu henclaur (I love a bit of this on rhubarb crumble, but I've never used one of these.)

_____

pstidick (Also found under a bonnet.)

_____

feir oshe (Firefighters make you wet with these.)

_____

fcpueolk (Gives a new meaning to pole dancing.)

_____

atme dor (Maybe you have one of these for your barbecue.)

_____

mtea sikct (If a dog fetched this it would probably eat it too.)

_____

irayh rancay (I've seen ones with feathers but never one like this.)

_____

niewer (Not only in Germany.)

_____

loev toncruehn (A romantic policeman maybe calls his this.)

_____

hdmooan (If you have a penis you are a …? If you haven't been circumcised then you will have one of these.)

_____

rhkigen (In London there is a building with this name. Imagine saying you work in a penis!)

_____

Joohnsn (Some guy's surname. He either wasn't liked or liked very much.)

_____

Jnoh Tashom (A poor guy who was named after a penis.)

_____

odl achp (Maybe because it can sometimes look like one.)

_____

oen-edey usetror nesak (Cyclops, location and animal.)

_____

ackepag (Amazon doesn't deliver this kind. Well I doubt it.)

_____

epe-epe (Kids love to double up words. I have never heard an adult use this one.)

_____

eecpi (In reference to a gun maybe?)

_____

Pteer (I've a few friends with this name.)

_____

pnki gacir (I don't smoke, but I wouldn't say no to this.)

_____

serpsi (Some people also use this as slang for the toilet.)

_____

pkor srdwo (Jewish people look away. The first word here should be kosher.)

_____

pytnho (But isn't one of these deadly?)

_____

slmiaa (Spicy or not? I wouldn't put it on my pizza.)

_____

wnga (There are many fish and chip shops with this word up in lights in the UK.)

_____

kisn teflu (For all your musical people out there.)

_____

gsasaue (Food again - thinking of cocks makes people hungry it seems.)

_____

sahft (Which to be honest is only part of the actually penis.)

_____

tdhir gle (When you want to be a tripod.)

_____

eoutrsr kemony (You must have some pretty baggy ones to fit one of these in.)

_____

tnghiy (We use this a lot in the English language when we don't remember the correct word. I've no idea how you can't remember at least one of these alter egos.)

_____

tgode (Rhymes with "lodge".)

_____

rat (This is also what covers roads.)

_____

THE VAGINA

Now you have shown your vast knowledge of many alternative names for a penis, try with the lady parts.

ehrinwispg eey (Can these even speak?)

_____

giwane (When you want it to sound more French.)

_____

bigonaj (Sounds like a board game. Shall we play it tonight?)

_____

ferowl (I have many of these on my roof.)

_____

dlay degarn (Also women have these too, not just me on my roof.)

_____

avg (This word is short and sweet and rhymes with the wife of Homer Simpson.)

_____

afnyn (In America this has a different meaning. There are also some people with this name.)

_____

tatw (Also used to insult people. Rhymes with a cute furry animal.)

_____

ohle (A man came up with this one for sure. Not to make this too confusing.)

_____

nutc (See you next Tuesday.)

_____

bxo (Doesn't have a lid but can contain things.)

_____

enpis yfl atrp (I had one of these but I didn't water it and it died. Oh wait! The first word is different.)

_____

ngiem (Remove a letter from the word that means a very unattractive person and change the pronunciation.)

_____

nlgfae (To me this sounds like a nice quiche.)

_____

nypta atherms (I had one of these, not in the same place, but he ate his way out to freedom.)

_____

pnki toac (Maybe this one originated from Mexico.)

_____

supsy (I love cuddling up with one or more of these on the sofa.)

_____

vayyjaja (This name sounds very spectacular. Please welcome on stage…)

_____

veraltic ilesm (Aren't they all?)

_____

hac cah (Let's do this together! 1,2,…)

_____

velo nneltu (Not the one between France and the UK.)

_____

hynoe otp (Winnie-the-Poo has one of these.)

_____

tuut (I am not a big fan of ballet.)

_____

ckieoo (What Americans call a biscuit.)

_____

fuinmf (Also this food has many names in different parts.)

_____

capkcue (It is very generous to take these to a new neighbour.)

_____

aben (Many of these can make you fart.)

_____

eeabvr (Yes, some people call it this too. I like the animal but don't see the similarity.)

_____

mffu (You can put these on your ears to keep them warm in winter.)

_____

frnot tombto (Another very location-based description.)

_____

tytki (Also a collection of money.)

_____

tpencupe (Old English money.)

_____

ahir epi (I'd send mine back to the kitchen.)

_____

ono oon (Before or after Teletubbies was created?)

_____

GETTING DOWN TO BUSINESS (SHAGGING)

Whether you are having sex or making love it all ends the same way, or should do.

There are many words which mean 'to have intercourse'.

True or False

Tick TRUE if you think the following mean 'to have sex' and tick FALSE if you think they don't.

	True	**False**
to bonk		
to fuck		
to screw		
to lay		
to roger		
to go at it		
to sleep with		
to bang		
to shag		
to get it on		

Did you get them all correct?

Let's take a look at some vocabulary that we need to know while this magic moment is going on. You don't want to misunderstand during a quickie.

What's a quickie? A quickie is a very fast sexual encounter. Obviously you all never have these, but at least now your vocabulary is expanding.

Here we have some words and expressions.

facefuck / top / bottom / active / passive / versatile / power bottom / bareback / BDSM / dirty talk / foreplay / hickey / feel up / cop off / meat and two veg / packing / bulge

How many do you know? Complete the sentences below with the correct word or expression. Be careful of the tenses! After all, this *is* an exercise book.

- Someone _____ me _____ on the bus on the way to work this morning.

- Sliding your cock in and out of a person's mouth is called _____.

- Did you know that _____ means the same as _____ and

_____ means the same as _____?

- I am _____. I am neither a top nor a bottom.

- His _____ is distracting me. He need to get looser pants!

- I heard Robert is a _____. His boyfriend doesn't need to do a thing.

- Last night I found out that Shelly is into _____. It was a bit of surprise when I saw her tied up.

- _____ and _____ are not the same thing. One is only words and the other isn't.

- Did you _____ at the party last night? Yes, with a guy who is _____!

- To make a _____ go down you could try putting toothpaste on it.

- A nice term for a guy's private parts is his _____.

- Be careful when having sex _____. Make sure you get regular tests.

So you have just learnt that 'meat and two veg' is a way of saying a man's private parts. There is also another very nice expression. I am sure people in royalty use this expression more than 'meat and two veg'. The expression is 'crown jewels'. This expression makes them sound very shiny, don't you think?

Still on the topic of getting down to business let's take a look at…

SEX POSITIONS

As I am sure you are well aware, there are certain sex positions which can be carried out no matter by what type of couple you are. Maybe scissoring is exclusive to lesbians but there are many we all share. With the aids of dildos or strap ons if you want a penis and don't have one, we can more or less try each and every amazing position.

Let's see if you can describe the following positions.

The corkscrew (Yes, I said cork and not cock this time. A corkscrew is what we use to get that pesky cork out of a bottle.)

_____

_____

_____

The face-off (Named after the television series? I doubt.)

_____

_____

_____

Doggy style (In some countries this position has different names. I especially find the Italian "sheep" translation quite cute.)

_____

_____

_____

The pretzel dip (Why is food always involved in one way or another?)

_____

_____

_____

The flatiron (Sounds like something you do around the house as a chore. Well it can be done around the house but it isn't housework.)

_____

_____

_____

The cross (For all you religious folk out there. Try this one. Jesus approves.)

_____

_____

_____

Bumper cars (I used to like riding these at the fair. I didn't know it was a sex position though.)

_____

_____

_____

A rusty trombone (If a trombone is rusty shouldn't you buy a new one?)

_____

_____

_____

Missionary (I think this one you all know.)

_____

_____

_____

MORE SEX POSITIONS

Unscramble the names.

The wings

The man lies on the floor and then lifts his hips up off the ground to make a bridge shape. His partner, male or female, can sit on top of him, legs either side as if standing but with a little stool - his cock.

The candedva ocw

Well, this doesn't sound like a compliment to me at all, but let me explain what it is. The cow position is actually when one partner stands facing away from the other with legs spread to give space for penetration, once inside, the person puts their hands on the floor and off you go. This position is the same but once their hands are on the floor the partner behind lifts the 'cow's' legs up around their waist. A lot of effort if you ask me.

The zAmnao

Yes, the 'a' is capital! Why? Maybe the famous company invented it or the delivery guys taught their customers it. Let your imaginations run wild. So, what is it? In this position one of the two is lay on their back on the floor while the other pushes up the legs of the person lay on the floor and then sits on their private parts. So the one on the floor is like a baby having their nappy changed but then the other partner decides to push their legs back a bit more and sit on them. And why not?

The gdoburady

Maybe Kevin Costner invented this one. It is where the receiver is standing and the giver is behind him/her. Like spooning in an upright position. This helps movement. You can do a lot more twisting, grinding and thrusting.

A psti asrto

Three are needed for this. One is in the middle like the kebab, let's say. The person in the middle performs oral sex on one person while he/her is being penetrated from behind. I know. Maybe for vegetarians we can call this a falafel roast?

Tae-gbngagi

Now this one I disagree with, the name I mean. You don't dip your teabag in and out of your boiling water, otherwise it will be a weak cuppa. But getting back to the sex position. This is when a man puts his bollocks into a person's mouth and takes them out, then back in again etc. See my problem with this? Or even slapping someone on the head with his testicles. Each to their own I guess (tea wise I mean!).

THE FIVE KNUCKLE SHUFFLE

No, this is not like a hand jive (for those who even know what that is), it is a way to say 'masturbating'. Now is the time to learn some more ways to say one of man's favourite past times.

Here you have some of the many alternative ways to say 'to masturbate'. See if you can *cum* up with the missing word.

1. spanking the _____

2. rubbing _____ out

3. tossing yourself _____

4. jerking yourself _____

5. choking the _____

6. beating the _____

7. making the _____ man cry

8. milking the _____

9. cuffing the _____

10. going on a _____ with Fisty Palmer

11. smacking the _____

12. evicting the _____ squatters

WORD SEARCH

How many terms for masturbating both for men and for women can you find in the word search below?

```
Z  G  P  R  A  C  T  I  C  E  S  E  L  F  A  B  U  S  E  D  V  L  K
E  F  L  I  C  K  T  H  E  B  E  A  N  F  B  C  U  L  J  O  E  C  Y
R  X  Q  M  W  I  Z  B  I  J  U  Z  Q  E  R  K  W  M  T  C  L  T  E
T  U  M  Q  N  Z  L  Z  Y  Q  F  N  C  C  A  U  S  Y  O  A  K  Z  K
V  A  R  N  I  S  H  T  H  E  F  L  A  G  P  O  L  E  S  T  C  Q  N
H  X  I  W  Z  M  H  R  Q  F  Q  G  L  G  F  K  K  W  S  E  I  A  O
F  K  F  Z  N  W  M  I  Q  V  N  M  M  F  N  Z  W  S  T  H  P  X  M
H  P  G  G  E  L  O  P  R  U  O  Y  E  N  I  H  S  H  H  T  E  D  E
N  H  M  T  J  Y  F  B  X  S  O  T  M  K  T  K  O  S  E  E  H  I  H
F  W  R  I  S  T  A  E  R  O  B  I  C  S  C  B  G  R  T  L  T  J  T
R  K  E  U  M  O  L  D  W  W  E  K  D  O  O  D  C  E  U  K  E  G  K
J  I  Q  E  N  M  L  I  G  L  M  A  G  T  I  R  N  E  R  C  L  Q  N
C  K  X  P  S  D  C  X  U  Y  N  S  C  G  N  V  A  H  K  I  K  A  A
Y  U  T  U  O  E  N  O  B  U  R  D  N  C  L  R  Q  I  E  T  C  Z  P
C  Q  P  D  M  Y  S  E  O  N  F  T  A  W  V  I  Y  T  Y  U  I  I  S
G  G  Z  P  A  V  B  B  S  Y  R  J  L  Z  D  P  T  R  J  S  T  A  W
```

41

GOING DOWN (LADIES FIRST)

Every time you step into a lift from now on and you hear the recorded voice saying, "Going down" you will enjoy the moment a little more.

'To go down' means to perform oral sex. This is just one of the many expressions we can use to say pleasuring your man or woman orally. Let's learn some more.

Ladies first. Here are some expressions which all mean going down on a woman. Can you complete them correctly?

Choose from the words below.

bed / canyon / carpet / Venus / teeth / eating / beard / fur / furry / out / ride / split / cunt / job / face

_____-munching

breakfast in _____

yodelling in the _____

whispering to _____

brushing one's _____

_____ at the "Y"

donning the _____

a _____ burger

drinking from the _____ cup

eating _____

a moustache _____

giving _____

a head _____

_____ lapping

a lickety _____

Yes, there are more. Choose the correct word from the choices given.

sitting/whistling in the dark

going *south/east*

flap/lip service

flicking/eating pussy

cock/bird-washing

sneezing in the *cabbage/cornflakes*

a box *lunch/supper*

eating a *peach/steak*

muff-*diving/surfing*

pruning the *orchid/jasmine*

playing the hair *harmonica/violing*

pearl-*diving/polishing*

shrimping/oysterying

a *skull/bone* job

wearing the *feed/shopping* bag

Are there more? There sure are. Have a look at the following which again all mean giving oral pleasure to a woman. Rearrange the letters in the word(s) to make them all correct?

parting the *ZFUZ*

_____

pussy-*INBBLNIG*

_____

a *TAUN* taco

_____

IARNBKG at the ape

_____

speaking in *TONSGUE*

_____

testing the *EHOC* in the love *VECA*

_____

tipping the *ELEVVT*

_____

TOUENG-fucking

_____

MIRINTMG the hedges

_____

NEARWIG the sticky *BREAD*

_____

whispering into the *ETW ARE*

_____

GOING DOWN (TIME FOR A BJ)

When I was at school I had a friend called B.J. Little did we know at that age what these two letters stood for. Obviously my friend's name wasn't Blow Job, but as time passed we all started to think it was. I wonder where he is now? Probably somewhere with a smile on his face.

Why is a blowjob called a blowjob and not a suck job? Well so people say, and as you know the internet is always correct, in the 17th century, well before any of us were born, to 'blow' meant to bring someone to orgasm.

What about giving head? Well to give head means to give a blow job. But are we talking about the head of the penis or the fact that your head is moving as you perform? To be honest - who cares?

See if you can find all the slang ways to say blow job in the word search.

Expressions to find

Addressing the court

Blowing the love whistle

Giving head

Cock-gobbling

Bone-lipping

Bobbing for apples

Face-frosting

Fluting

Gobbling pork

Giving brain

Head job

Licking the lollipop

Kneeling at the alter

Mouth-fucking

Mouth-milking

Skull-buggery

Sucking off

```
H K B D C H B Y T E P L Y J A Y M H X W J S B
S M Y L A W G O B B L I N G P O R K J T S V O
K B O N E L I P P I N G E R R Q Z V E B S Z B
U J Y T H I A Y W C C J F S N F X Q K R P J B
L F I D R E T L A E H T T A G N I L E E N K I
L N P O P I L L O L E H T G N I K C I L B N N
B I B O J D A E H J U V Z I O Y A C R T B N G
U A D D R E S S I N G T H E C O U R T H O J F
G R U E H Z N J E Y C K R M J Z I V Z Q L S O
G B I R I J U Z G N I L B B O G K C O C E Y R
E G Q Q H I T I A G N I T U L F J A M G A D A
R N X M E F F O G N I K C U S H Z M L K A J P
Y I A E T S U M O U T H M I L K I N G X N P
Y V K Q I N I G I V I N G H E A D M V N E C L
C I Q I C P K G V P Y I X D B O L B O W N Y E
H G S N J J K F A C E F R O S T I N G Y D E S
```

SEX PHRASAL VERBS

Match the sex phrasal verbs to their definition.

to get it on / to sleep around / to hit on / to jizz on / to cheat on / to cum on / to pull out /
to feel someone up / to suck off /

_____	to fondle someone for sexual pleasure
_____	to ejaculate on
_____	to remove your penis before you ejaculate
_____	to have sex
_____	to perform oral sex on a man
_____	to ejaculate on
_____	to have sex with many different people
_____	to make sexual advances towards someone
_____	to have an affair

CUT OR UNCUT?

As we are all fully aware boys are born with foreskin, but some people decide to be circumcised. This means there are two types of penis out there - the ones with and the ones without. Can you figure out which of the expressions below refer to a circumcised penis or an un-circumcised penis?

HUNGARIAN SAUSAGE / CUT / UNCUT / CANADIAN BACON /
CHOPPED AND SCREWED / CHANGE PURSE / TURTLE NECK / ROUNDHEAD /
CUT LUNCH / CHICKEN NECK / GOY TOY / HOODLESS COBRA /
COLLARLESS MUSHROOM / KOSHER SALAMI / HOODED WARRIOR / KENNY / WIZARD'S HAT

Circumcised	Un-circumcised

MORNING GLORY

There are many words and expressions we can use when referring to an erection.
There are also many words and expressions we can use when referring to semen.
See if you can guess which of the following refer to an erection and which to semen.

*LOB-ON / JIZZ / CREAM / STIFFY / WOODIE / MORNING GLORY / HARD-ON / CUM / MILK /
SPUNK / WAD / SEED / LOAD /WOOD / PITCHING A TENT / BONER*

Erection	Semen

VOCABULARY QUIZ

Match the word or expression to its definition.

POSTBONED / CREAMPIE / AFTERCARE / EDGING / BOOFING / BLUE BALLS / BUSSY /
DOPPELBANGER / FELTCHING / MASTUWAITING / DEEP THROATING

Like with old people or after an operation, this is when you make sure everyone is feeling comfortable after what just went on in your bedroom.

This sounds cute, but I guess could be quite dangerous. This is when your partner puts drugs into your anus either using their finger or putting it on the end of their penis / strap on, whatever you have handy.

A combination of the word 'boy' and 'pussy' meaning a boy's anus. Used quite a lot in the gay world.

I know there are some of you out there who would dream of having sex with yourself. All those who spend hours in front of the mirror masturbating looking into your own eyes. Well, now is your chance because this means to have sex with someone who looks like you!

This is when your partner drinks his cum out of your anus after having anal sex and shooting his load up there. Can be done with a straw or without. Save plastic and do without!

This makes me laugh. This is when you are wanking off and the video you are watching has stuck due to lack of internet connection or your VHS tape has jammed (if you even know what one of those is.) So you have to hold back from cumming.

_____

I really hope my computer doesn't use these new words when suggesting auto-correction. This one could get you into a bit of a pickle with the boss. Sorry I will be … Pay attention. This means you are running late because you were just having a quickie with someone somewhere.

_____

No, you haven't been sitting in the snow naked for too long even if maybe you would prefer that to the actual meaning. This term refers to the sheer pain, excruciating pain of stopping yourself from cumming during sexual arousal.

_____

Sounds tasty, right? I always say desserts should be full of something wet otherwise what is the point? Am I right? Well this word is used to describe when your semen is dripping out of your partner's vagina or anus after getting down to business.

_____

Personally I gag at the thought of anything touching my tonsils but this action refers to taking as much of a man's penis into your mouth and throat as possible. Some people can actually fit it all in! Either congrats to the person doing this or commiserations to the man with the small weapon. It's not the size, it's what you can do with it. So they say. Who are *they*?

_____

This is also something you can do in your garden, but I strongly recommend against doing the sexual version in your garden unless you live miles from anyone or can't be seen. Then maybe… maybe. This is when you delay your partner's orgasm for as long as possible. You keep arousing them over and over, but always making sure they don't orgasm or cum. Note how I said both, because yes, men can cum without an orgasm! Sad, but true. This can also be part of a bondage game or just sat on the sofa. The aim of this 'fun' activity is to make the climax even better.

TYPES OF GAY MEN

Did you know that there are many different types of gay men? Down to every fine detail. Yes, some people say that types shouldn't be used, but as long as you use them in an endearing way you shouldn't offend anyone.

Are you an otter or a bear? Is your neighbour a spunk monkey or a pup? Do you have any idea what I am talking about?

Below are just a few of the types of gay men that are out there. See if you can match the type of gay man to the correct description.

POZ-FRIENDLY / DADDY / OTTER /SPUNK MONKEY / GYM BUNNY / HOXTON QUEER / CUB / BEAR / CHUB / JOCK / MUSCLE BEAR / PUP / WOLF / TWINK / POLAR BEAR / CHASER / PANDA / DISCREET / POZ

_____   A guy over 30 who has a heavier build, usually hairy.

_____   Someone in his late 20s -30s. Used for young bears. Sometimes this is used to say that someone is the passive partner in a relationship.

_____   A on-the-heavy-side guy. Some could say overweight. Not very hairy.

_____   Athletic to muscular build, usually had their hair removed so they look like dolphins. Late 20s-30s.

_____   An arty person. Doesn't matter what shape he is or how muscular he is.

_____   Again late 20s-30s. Why is it this age group has so many types? Obsessed with the gym. Muscular. Again probably without hair.

_____   Same as a bear but with muscles. Their size is usually down to muscle not fat. May have their hair trimmed in a way to show off their body shape.

_____   Lean guys. Again late 20s-30s. Usually hairy.

_____   Again late 20s-30s. Can be lean or muscular.

_____   Someone who gets excited easily around other men.

_____   Late teens to early 20s. Very boyish looking. Thin or slim.

_____ Late 30s to 40s. Lean but can also be slightly muscular. With hair.

_____ An older bear with white hair.

_____ Someone who is attracted to bears or cubs but isn't part of the culture.

_____ An Asian bear.

_____ A man who has to be discreet. Maybe he is in a relationship or not out of the closet.

_____ A HIV positive man who doesn't hide his status.

_____ A person willing to have sex with someone who is HIV positive even if he is not.

_____ An older guy who generally likes younger men.

TYPES OF GAY MEN (yes, there are more!)

ACROSS

1. A gay man who likes to flirt with many different guys and probably sleep with them too. (2 words)
3. A gay guy with a nice body but is ugly. Like shrimp. You don't pay attention to the face when you are eating one, do you?
5. An older guy who looks for young boys to have sex with. (2 words)
7. The same as a gym bunny. Someone who wants to stay at the gym 24 hours a day in order to look ripped. He is always talking about the gym. (2 words)
8. A man who is into kinky sexual activities.
9. A gay man who says that he is now straight even if it is not true.
13. A slim, athletic, hairless bear.
14. A person who has just come out of the closet. (2 words)

DOWN

2. A guy who goes around bars trying to hook up with other people's partners. (2 words)
3. An attractive man with grey hair. (2 words)
4. A young gay guy who prefers older men. (2 words)
6. A young gay man.
7. A gay asian.
10. A muscular twink.
11. An extremely muscular gay guy.
12. A gamer who is homosexual.

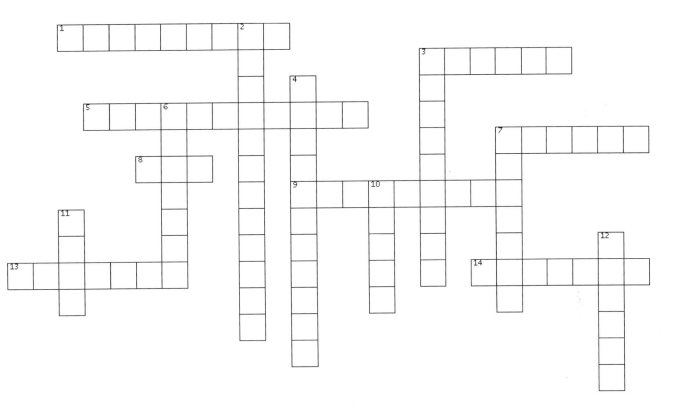

TYPES OF GAY WOMEN

Yes, maybe you didn't know but there are also different types of gay women out there. They don't all know how to fix your radiator.
See if you can put in the missing letters to reveal the correct answers.

A li__sti__k lesbian	These lesbians dress in a very feminine and girly way. Sometimes over the top. Hoops, big hair etc.
A __ut__h lesbian	Tough looking, without make-up, masculine.
A c__ap__tick lesbian	Likes dressing up but not as much as the lipstick lesbian and not as butch as a butch lesbian. She is also happy in just t-shirt and jeans to feel comfy.
An al__ha lesbian	Very attractive, perfect style, too cool for school. Someone very powerful and popular.
A s__o__e butch lesbian	The same as a butch lesbian but she is a giver. This woman wants her partner to be the receiver of pleasure. A giver.
A __ill__w prin__ess lesbian	A lesbian who prefers to receive sexual pleasure rather than give it.
A s__ort__y lesbian	A lesbian in love with sports.
A lo__e s__ar lesbian	A lesbian who tried to have sex with a man just once.
A __o__d star lesbian	A lesbian who has never had sex with a man.
A __as__ian lesbian	Was a lesbian but now dates men.
A __o__er lesbian	Someone who is in control of her life and work. Always the best at what she does. Top of the top.
A ba__y d__ke	A lesbian who has just come out of the closet.
A s__ __d lesbian	A lesbian of black or latin descent. Dominant and masculine.
An ac__ivi__t lesbian	This type of lesbian has a strong passion for social justice. This person doesn't stand out for any specific reason like other types of lesbians. Her passion for justice makes her an inspiration.

VOCABULARY QUIZ 2

Fill in the missing letters and match the words and expressions to their definitions.

*SN_O_LING / MI_ _-HI_ _ CLUB / RI_ _ING / G_ _DEN D_CKIN_ /
S_OW_ALLIN_ / G_L_EN S_O_ER /
M_ _OR_ _ATING / JE_ _ING / C_ _ _MY TU_ _LE / D_ _KING*

_____

Also known as the double dolphin, this activity is done between two men. One must be circumcised and one not. The uncircumcised man rolls his foreskin over the head of the circumcised man's penis.

_____

This comes under 'water sports'. No not surfing, the sexual kind. This term refers to when one partner pisses on, in front of or near the other.

_____

Put that penis pump away, you don't need it anymore if you believe this words. This is the exercise of stroking, like a cat, your cock while you have a hard-on in order to make it bigger.

_____

If you are member of this you have never flown on Ryanair, the toilets are too small! You become a member of this not-so-exclusive club if you manage to have sex above the clouds. So who was the founder? Mary Poppins of course!

_____

First docking must take place. Then after docking is completed (sounds like an episode of Star Trek) the circumcised man urinates inside his partner's foreskin until there is an explosion.

_____

Do you remember when you were a child and you used to make the noise of trains, planes and cars? Try putting your head between your partner's breasts, moving it from side to side and making the sound of this luxurious form of transport.

—————————————————

Mouth to anus contact. There are many of you out there who say "How disgusting!" but have you actually tried it? I say, these things are like salad dressings. You need to try them all before you decide which you like. I'm not saying your anus tastes of a salad dressing, but you get my point. Try all these things before you say you don't like it. I am sure if you try this one you will.

—————————————————

My father used to have fights with these things with my classmates. But this term is a sexual term, not the play fighting term. Thankfully! I'd need to speak to my psychiatrist after if he had been doing this with all the kids from my school. This term refers to one person with a penis cumming into his partner's mouth and then they pass it back and forth between each other's mouths while kissing. Seems like a challenge more than fun. Like an adult egg and spoon race.

—————————————————

How sweet and romantic does this sound? This is when two men rub the ends of their penises together to arouse one another. Still sounds sweet though.

—————————————————

This can be done after snoodling. This is when the circumcised man ejaculates into the non-circumcised man's foreskin.

QUIZ: TRUE OR FALSE?

1. To beat off also means to masturbate?   T/F

2. Flicking the bean is not actually advised by doctors as it can cause harm.   T/F

3. Headaches can make you more in the mood for sex.   T/F

4. Your orgasm will be better if you leave your socks on.   T/F

5. There are 36 calories in a teaspoon of semen.   T/F

6. The average female orgasm lasts one minute whereas in men only 6 seconds.   T/F

7. Masturbating daily reduces a man's sperm count.   T/F

8. There are some sex positions that stop you from getting pregnant.   T/F

9. Put away the placenta masks, start using sperm masks. Sperm has anti-wrinkle properties.   T/F

10. Fetuses can get hard ons.   T/F

11. A man has on average eleven erections a day.   T/F

12. Smoking can't shrink your penis.   T/F

13. When you are aroused you can stand more pain.   T/F

14. The UK first allowed LGBTQIA+ couples to adopt in 2020.   T/F

15. Women have two kinds of orgasms. One is vaginal and one is clitoral.   T/F

ENJOY!

Answers

Challenge 1

1. Glans
2. Foreskin
3. Shaft
4. Veins
5. Pubic hair / pubes (shaved!)
6. Scrotum / ballsack

Challenge 2

1. Bladder
2. Prostate gland
3. Urethra
4. Epididymis
5. Testicle

Challenge 3

1. Hand
2. Clitoris
3. Urethral opening
4. Labia minora
5. Labia majora
6. Vaginal opening
7. Perineo
8. Anus

Challenge 4

1. Fallopian tube
2. Ovary
3. Uterus
4. Cervix
5. Vagina

The Cock

dick
prick
member
tool
knob
maypole
dong
winkle
willy
joystick
weapon
pocket rocket
pecker
tadger
schlong
widgie
meat
love muscle
wick
love stick
custard launcher
dipstick
fire hose
fuckpole
meat rod
meat stick
hairy canary
wiener
love truncheon
manhood
gherkin
Johnson
John Thomas
old chap
one-eyed trouser snake
package
pee-pee
piece
Peter
pink cigar
pisser
pork sword
python

salami
wang
skin flute
sausage
shaft
third leg
trouser monkey
thingy
todge
tar

The Vagina

whispering eye
vagine
bajingo
flower
lady garden
vag
fanny
twat
hole
cunt
box
penis fly trap
minge
flange
panty hamster
pink taco
pussy
vajayjay
vertical smile
cha cha
love tunnel
honey pot
tutu
cookie
muffin
cupcake
bean
beaver
muff
front bottom
kitty

tuppence
hair pie
noo noo

Getting down to business (shagging)

True or False
All true

Someone <u>felt me up</u> on the bus on the way to work this morning.
Sliding your cock in and out of a person's mouth is called <u>facefucking</u>.
Did you know that <u>active</u> means the same as <u>top</u> and <u>passive</u> means the same as <u>bottom</u>?
I am <u>versatile</u>. I am neither a top nor a bottom.
His <u>bulge</u> is distracting me. He need to get looser pants!
I heard Robert is a <u>power bottom</u>. His boyfriend doesn't need to do a thing.
Last night I found out that Shelly is into <u>BDSM</u>. It was a bit of surprise when I saw her tied up.
<u>Dirty talk</u> and <u>foreplay</u> are not the same thing. One is only words and the other isn't.
Did you <u>cop off</u> at the party last night? Yes, with a guy who is <u>packing</u>!
To make a <u>hickey</u> go down you could try putting toothpaste on it.
A nice term for a guy's private parts is his <u>meat and two veg</u>.
Be careful when having sex <u>bareback</u>. Make sure you get regular tests.

Sex positions

The Corkscrew
The man or woman with a strap-on lays flat on their back with their erection pointing up to the ceiling. The female climbs on top inserted the penis into her vagina and spins around 360 degrees. Like a corkscrew. The woman then can jump off just before the man cums everywhere like popping the cork off a bottle of champagne.

The face-off
One of the couple has to sit on the edge of a sofa, chair or bed with their feet on the ground but legs spread slightly. The other person gets onto their partner's lap, face to face. Their legs wrapped around their partner's waist or hips.

Doggy style
One partner is penetrated from behind by the other while supporting themselves on their hands and knees like a dog.

The pretzel dip
One partner lies on their side as the other straddles their lower leg (the one on the bed for example, keeping their torso upright. The person who is lay on their side bends the higher leg as the straddling partner thrusts into the person.

The flatiron
One partner lies flat down on their stomach while the other straddles the back of their partner's thighs and then penetrates from behind.

The cross
The name comes from the fact that the couple forms a T shape whilst carrying out this position. The penetrating partner lies on their side while the receiver lies perpendicular raising their legs to allow the penis to enter. Once penetration has occurred the receiver lowers their legs finishing off the cross shape. This can also be used for anal sex.

Bumper cars
A position for anal sex. Both partners lie belly down facing away from each other, legs spread, arms in front of your head, as if swimming or you can rest on your elbows. Make sure the penetrating partner is on top. Then you slowly back into each other until the penis or strap on enters. This can be tricky but patience is a virtue.

A rusty trombone
This is when one partner is rimming and masturbating the other at the same time. Like playing a trombone.

Missionary
The missionary position is when the man lies on top of the woman and they are facing each other. It gets it name from the fact that missionaries thought it was the 'proper' position for primitive people.

More Sex Positions

The swing
The advanced cow
The Amazon
The bodyguard
A spit roast
Tea-bagging

The five knuckle shuffle

1. spanking the monkey
2. rubbing one out
3. tossing yourself off
4. jerking yourself off
5. choking the chicken
6. beating the bishop
7. making the bald man cry
8. milking the cow
9. cuffing the carrot
10. going on a date with Fisty Palmer
11. smacking the salami
12. evicting the testicular squatters

Word search

```
. . P R A C T I C E S E L F A B U S E . . . .
. F L I C K T H E B E A N . . . . . . O E . Y
. . . . . . . . . . . . . . . . . . T C L . E
. . . . . . . . . . . . . . . . . O A K . K
V A R N I S H T H E F L A G P O L E S T C . N
. . . . . . . . . . . . . . . . . S E I . O
. . . . . . . . . . . . . . . . T H P . M
. . . . . E L O P R U O Y E N I H S . H T E . E
. . . . . . . . . . . . . . . . E E H . H
. W R I S T A E R O B I C S . . . T L T . T
. . . . . . . . . . . . . . . . U K E . K
. . . . . . . . . . . . . . . . R C L . N
. . . . . . . . . . . . . . . . K I K . A
. . T U O E N O B U R . . . . . . E T C . P
. . . . . . . . . . . . . . . . Y . I . S
. . . . . . . . . . . . . . . . . T . . .
```

Going down

carpet-munching
breakfast in bed
yodelling in the canyon
whispering to Venus
brushing one's teeth
eating at the "Y"
donning the beard
a furburger
drinking from the furry cup
eating out
a moustache ride
giving face
a head job
cunt lapping
a lickety split
whistling in the dark
going south
lip service
eating pussy
bird-washing
sneezing in the cabbage
a box lunch
eating a peach
muff-diving
pruning the orchid
playing the hair harmonica
pearl-diving
shrimping
a skull job
wearing the feed bag
parting the fuzz
pussy-nibbling
a tuna taco
barking at the ape
speaking in tongues
testing the echo in the love cave
tipping the velvet
tongue-fucking
trimming the hedges
wearing the sticky beard
whispering into the wet ear

Going down (time for a BJ)

```
.   .   .   .   .   .   .   .   .   .   .   .   .   .   .   .   .   .   .   .   B
S   .   .   .   .   .   G   O   B   B   L   I   N   G   P   O   R   K   .   .   .   .   O
K   B   O   N   E   L   I   P   P   I   N   G   .   .   .   .   .   .   .   .   .   B
U   .   .   .   .   .   .   .   .   .   .   .   .   .   .   .   .   .   .   .   .   .   B
L   .   .   .   R   E   T   L   A   E   H   T   T   A   G   N   I   L   E   E   N   K   I
L   N   P   O   P   I   L   L   O   L   E   H   T   G   N   I   K   C   I   L   .   .   N
B   I   B   O   J   D   A   E   H   .   .   .   .   .   .   .   .   .   .   .   .   G
U   A   D   D   R   E   S   S   I   N   G   T   H   E   C   O   U   R   T   .   .   .   F
G   R   .   .   .   .   .   .   .   .   .   .   .   .   .   .   .   .   .   .   .   .   O
G   B   .   .   .   .   .   .   G   N   I   L   B   B   O   G   K   C   O   C   .   .   R
E   G   .   .   .   .   .   .   .   G   N   I   T   U   L   F   .   .   .   .   .   .   A
R   N   .   .   .   F   F   O   G   N   I   K   C   U   S   .   .   .   .   .   .   P
Y   I   .   .   .   .   .   M   O   U   T   H   M   I   L   K   I   N   G   .   .   .   P
.   V   .   .   .   .   .   G   I   V   I   N   G   H   E   A   D   .   .   .   .   .   L
.   I   .   .   .   .   .   .   .   .   .   .   .   .   .   .   .   .   .   .   .   E
.   G   .   .   .   .   .   F   A   C   E   F   R   O   S   T   I   N   G   .   .   .   S
```

Sex phrasal verbs

to feel someone up	to fondle someone for sexual pleasure
to jizz on	to ejaculate on
to pull out	to remove your penis before you ejaculate
to get it on	to have sex
to suck off	to perform oral sex on a man
to cum on	to ejaculate on
to sleep around	to have sex with many different people
to hit on	to make sexual advances towards someone
to cheat on	to have an affair

Cut or uncut?

Circumcised	Un-circumcised
cut	uncut
chopped and screwed	Canadian Bacon
roundhead	change purse
cut lunch	chicken neck
hoodless cobra	goy toy
collarless mushroom	hooded warrior
kosher salami	Hungarian sausage
	Kenny
	Wizard's hat
	turtle neck

Morning glory

Erection	Semen
hard-on	cum
morning glory	milk
boner	spunk
pitching a tent	wad
wood	seed
woodie	load
stiffy	cream
lob-on	jizz

Vocabulary Quiz

Aftercare
Like with old people or after an operation, this is when you make sure everyone is feeling comfortable after what just went on in your bedroom.

Boofing
This sounds cute, but I guess could be quite dangerous. This is when your partner puts drugs into your anus either using their finger or putting it on the end of their penis / strap on, whatever you have handy.

Bussy
A combination of the word 'boy' and 'pussy' meaning a boy's anus. Used quite a lot in the gay world.

Doppelbanger
I know there are some of you out there who would dream of having sex with yourself. All those who spend hours in front of the mirror masturbating looking into your own eyes. Well, now is your chance because this means to have sex with someone who looks like you!

Feltching
This is when your partner drinks his cum out of your anus after having anal sex and shooting his load up there. Can be done with a straw or without. Save plastic and do without!

Mastuwaiting
This makes me laugh. This is when you are wanking off and the video you are watching has stuck due to lack of internet connection or your VHS tape has jammed (if you even know what one of those is.) So you have to hold back from cumming.

Postboned
I really hope my computer doesn't use these new words when suggesting auto-correction. This one could get you into a bit of a pickle with the boss. Sorry I will be … Pay attention. This means you are running late because you were just having a quickie with someone somewhere.

Blue balls
No, you haven't been sitting in the snow naked for too long even if maybe you would prefer that to the actual meaning. This term refers to the sheer pain, excruciating pain of stopping yourself from cumming during sexual arousal.

Creampie
Sounds tasty, right? I always say desserts should be full of something wet otherwise what is the point? Am I right? Well this word is used to describe when your semen is dripping out of your partner's vagina or anus after getting down to business.

Deep throating

Personally I gag at the thought of anything touching my tonsils but this term, this action refers to taking as much of a man's penis into your mouth and throat as possible. Some people can actually fit it all it! Either congrats to the person doing this or commiserations to the man with the small weapon. It's not the size, it's what you can do with it. So they say. Who are *they*?

Edging

This is also something you can do in your garden, but I strongly recommend against doing the sexual version in your garden unless you live miles from anyone or can't be seen. Then maybe… maybe. This is when you delay your partner's orgasm for as long as possible. You keep arousing them over and over, but always making sure they don't orgasm or cum. Note how I said both, because yes, men can cum without an orgasm! Sad, but true. This can also be part of a bondage game or just sat on the sofa. The aim of this 'fun' activity is to make the climax even better.

Types of gay men

Bear	A guy over 30 who has a heavier build, usually hairy.
Cub	Someone in his late 20s -30s. Used for young bears. Sometimes this is used to say that someone is the passive partner in a relationship.
Chub	A on-the-heavy-side guy. Some could say overweight. Not very hairy.
Gym bunny	Athletic to muscular build, usually had their hair removed so they look like dolphins. Late 20s-30s.
Hoxton Queer	An arty person. Doesn't matter what shape he is or how muscular he is.
Jock	Again late 20s-30s. Why is it this age group has so many types? Obsessed with the gym. Muscular. Again probably without hair.
Muscle Bear	Same as a bear but with muscles. Their size is usually down to muscle not fat. May have their hair trimmed in a way to show off their body shape.
Otter	Lean guys. Again late 20s-30s. Usually hairy.
Pup	Again late 20s-30s. Can be lean or muscular.
Spunk Monkey	Someone who gets excited easily around other men.
Twink	Late teens to early 20s. Very boyish looking. Thin or slim.
Wolf	Late 30s to 40s. Lean but can also be slightly muscular. With hair.
Polar bear	An older bear with white hair.
Chaser	Someone who is attracted to bears or cubs but isn't part of the culture.
Panda	An Asian bear.
Discreet	A man who has to be discreet. Maybe he is in a relationship or not out of the closet.
Poz	A HIV positive man who doesn't hide his status.
Poz-friendly	A person willing to have sex with someone who is HIV positive even if he is not.
Daddy	An older guy who generally likes younger men.

Types of gay men (yes, there are more!)

ACROSS
1. Butterfly
3. Shrimp
5. Chicken hawk
7. Gym rat
8. Pig
9. Yestergay
13. Dolphin
14. Baby gay

DOWN
2. Lounge lizard
3. Silver fox
4. Daddy chaser
6. Chicken
7. Gaysian
10. Twunk
11. Bull
12. Gaymer

Types of gay women

A lipstick lesbian	These lesbians dress in a very feminine and girly way. Sometimes over the top. Hoops, big hair etc.
A butch lesbian	Tough looking, without make-up, masculine.
A chapstick lesbian	Likes dressing up but not as much as the lipstick lesbian and not as butch as a butch lesbian. She is also happy in just t-shirt and jeans to feel comfy.
An alpha lesbian	Very attractive, perfect style, too cool for school. Someone very powerful and popular.
A stone butch lesbian	The same as a butch lesbian but she is a giver. This woman wants her partner to be the receiver of pleasure. A giver.
A pillow princess lesbian	A lesbian who prefers to receive sexual pleasure rather than give it.
A sporty lesbian	A lesbian in love with sports.
A lone star lesbian	A lesbian who tried to have sex with a man just once.
A gold star lesbian	A lesbian who has never had sex with a man.
A hasbian lesbian	Was a lesbian but now dates men.
A power lesbian	Someone who is in control of her life and work. Always the best at what she does. Top of the top.
A baby dyke	A lesbian who has just come out of the closet.
A stud lesbian	A lesbian of black or latin descent. Dominant and masculine.
An activist lesbian	This type of lesbian has a strong passion for social justice. This person doesn't stand out for any specific reason like other types of lesbians. Her passion for justice makes her an inspiration.

Vocabulary Quiz 2

Docking

Also known as the double dolphin, this activity is done between two men. One must be circumcised and one not. The uncircumcised man rolls his foreskin over the head of the circumcised man's penis.

Golden shower

This comes under 'water sports'. No not surfing, the sexual kind. This term refers to when one partner pisses on, in front of or near the other.

Jelqing

Put that penis pump away, you don't need it anymore if you believe this words. This is the exercise of stroking, like a cat, your cock while you have a hard-on in order to make it bigger.

Mile-High Club

If you are member of this you have never flown on Ryanair, the toilet's are too small! You become a member of this not-so-exclusive club if you manage to have sex above the clouds. So who was the founder? Mary Poppins of course!

Golden docking

First docking must take place. Then after docking is completed (sounds like an episode of Star Trek) the circumcised man urinates inside his partner's foreskin until there is an explosion.

Motorboating

Do you remember when you were a child and you used to make the noise of trains, planes and cars? Try putting your head between your partner's breasts, moving it from side to side and making the sound of this luxurious form of transport.

Rimming

Mouth to anus contact. There are many of you out there who say "How disgusting!" but have you actually tried it? I say, these things are like salad dressings. You need to try them all before you decide which you like. I'm not saying your anus tastes of a salad dressing, but you get my point. Try all these things before you say you don't like it. I am sure if you try this one you will.

Snowballing

My father used to have fights with these things with my classmates. But this term is a sexual term, not the play fighting term. Thankfully! I'd need to speak to my psychiatrist after if he has been doing this with all the kids from my school. This term refers to one person with a penis cumming into his partner's mouth and then they pass it back and forth between each other's mouths while kissing. Seems like a challenge more than fun. Like an adult egg and spoon race.

Snoodling

How sweet and romantic does this sound? This is when two men rub the ends of their penises together to arouse one another. Still sounds sweet though.

Creamy turtle
This can be done after snoodling. This is when the circumcised man ejaculates into the non-circumcised man's foreskin.

Quiz: True or false?

1T, 2T, 3T, 4T, 5T, 6F (The average female orgasm lasts 20 seconds. That is 14 seconds more than the average man's orgasm), 7T, 8F (Absolutely not true!), 9T, 10T, 11T, 12F (It is true that smoking can cause your penis to shrink), 13T, 14F (It was in 2002), 15T.

Printed in Great Britain
by Amazon

14336209R00045

Ferry
&Cruise
2014

G000109148

Ferry
Publications

Published by:
Ferry Publications, PO Box 33, Ramsey, Isle of Man IM99 4LP
Tel: +44 (0) 1624 898445   Fax: +44 (0) 1624 898449
E-mail: ferrypubs@manx.net   Website: www.ferrypubs.co.uk

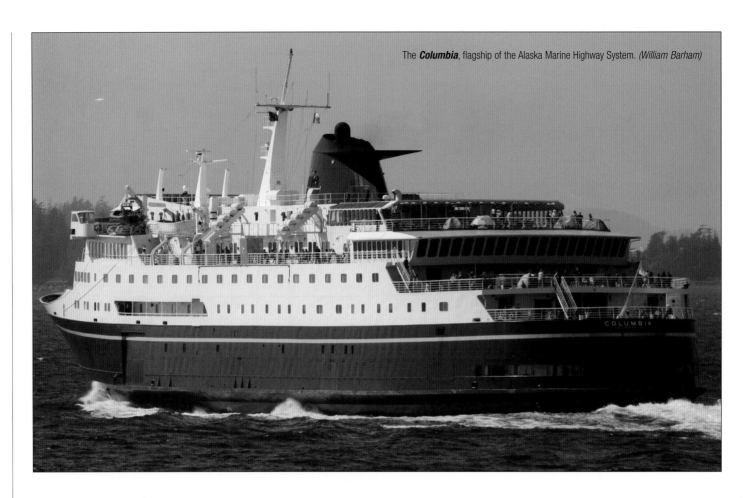
The *Columbia*, flagship of the Alaska Marine Highway System. *(William Barham)*

Contents

Produced and designed by Ferry Publications trading as Lily Publications Ltd
PO Box 33, Ramsey, Isle of Man, British Isles, IM99 4LP
Tel: +44 (0) 1624 898446   Fax: +44 (0) 1624 898449
www.ferrypubs.co.uk   E-Mail: info@lilypublications.co.uk

Editorial

The sixth edition of our annual *Ferry & Cruise* yearbook is again filled with a variety of specialist articles aimed to provide plenty of interest, satisfaction and visual pleasure to all followers of the passenger ship scene. Whether your delight is the modern and the large or the old and the small, all tastes are again catered for.

Anniversaries provide one theme for this edition. We closely look at the development and growth of Estonian operators Tallink who celebrate their quarter-century of service whilst a second article concentrates on their Tallinn-Helsinki service across the Gulf of Finland.

A further 50th anniversary relates to the former Southern Railway's turbine steamer *Isle of Thanet* which finished service at Folkestone in September 1963. Dating from 1925, the ship served an illustrious career while another, much smaller, vessel built in the previous year, continues to give much pleasure to her many followers and devotees. The diminutive paddle steamer *Kingswear Castle* was moved from the Medway to the River Dart in 2013 and we are happy to celebrate her return to the river on which she was built.

In Norway we review the sad loss of the Coastal Express steamer *Sanct Svithun* in 1962 while in the warmer south, we visit the ferries which served in the Aegean some 15 years ago as well as looking at the present day scene in the Canary Islands.

Other Photo Features visit the bustling port of Istanbul and its extensive passenger routes linking Europe with Asia, the vital but ageing fleet of the Alaska Marine Highway System (also 50 years old) and Saga's popular cruise ship *Saga Sapphire*.

The modern cruise ships *Norwegian Breakaway* and *Europa 2* have both created much interest and publicity since appearing in 2013 and their entry into service is celebrated with detailed reviews of both vessels. Both are very much products of their times, the former a huge floating resort catering for the demanding American market, the latter, smaller and more restrained and the first cruise ship to boast Safe Return To Port (SRTP) technology.

In the ferry world, the influence of the Channel Tunnel continues to cause repercussions with yet another company folding during 2013. An in depth piece concerning the influences of the tunnel on the ferry industry provides much fascinating material whilst the evolution of corporate branding on ferry exteriors is examined for the first time.

As usual we aim to provide something for everyone and it is to be hoped that the *2014 Ferry & Cruise* yearbook finds a valued space on the shelves of all those who profess to have an interest in passenger ships and the sea.

The Southern Railway's turbine steamer **Isle of Thanet** served for a magnificent 38 years until her withdrawal in September 1963. *(FotoFlite)*

1 Tallink and the Helsinki-Tallinn Line
by Kalle Id

The Estonian ferry operator Tallink celebrates its 25th anniversary in 2014. During this quarter of a century, the company has developed from operating a single second-hand ship between Helsinki and Tallinn into one of the largest ferry operators in the world.

FORMATION

Tallink was originally established in 1989 as a Soviet-Finnish joint venture. The two participant companies were Palkkiyhtymä of Finland and the Estonian Shipping Company (ESCO). Interestingly, at this point ESCO had already operated ferries between Helsinki and Tallinn for over two decades.

Estonskoje Morskoje Parokhodstvo, as ESCO was originally known in Russian, was established in 1960 as a subsidiary of the Baltic Shipping Company. In 1965, ESCO began passenger operations between Helsinki and Tallinn with the small steamer *Vanemuine*. The next year ESCO achieved a monopoly on the route, when the Finland Steamship Company (Finska Ångfartygs Aktiebolaget, FÅA) abandoned their Helsinki-Tallinn service. In 1968, the *Vanemuine* was replaced by the larger 1960-built *Tallinn* (ex *Svanetiya*), a 3,290 gross register ton motor ship with a capacity for 250 passengers. The *Tallinn* was the sole ship on the route until 1980 when the new *Georg Ots* (9,841 gross tons, 600 passengers, 340 cabin berths, 14 cars) arrived from a Polish shipyard.

In 1985, the status of the Helsinki-Tallinn route begun to change soon after Mikhail Gorbachev assumed the leadership of the Soviet Union when he passed the 'perestroika' and 'glasnost' reforms that gave more rights and freedoms to the Soviet citizens. At the same time ESCO started looking for a Finnish partner with which to form a new Helsinki-Tallinn ferry operator. After failed negotiations with Rederi Ab Eckerö, ESCO formed a joint venture, Tallink, with Palkkiyhtymä Oy in May 1989.

In December 1989 Tallink acquired its first ferry in the form of the *Tallink*, originally the Helsinki-Stockholm ferry *Svea Regina*. The 10,341 gross ton ferry entered service in January 1990, sailing under the Finnish flag and crewed by Finnlines. She had a capacity for 1,090 passengers, 410 cabin berths and 150 cars. During the first year, the *Tallink* made three 24-hour round trips from Helsinki to Tallinn per week. Despite the arrival of the new ship, the *Georg Ots* continued sailing on the route in competition.

The year 1990 saw a proliferation of new operators appear on the Helsinki-Tallinn line. The real boom came after Estonia declared independence from the Soviet Union in August 1991. Soon afterwards ESCO increased their ownership in Tallink to 71 per cent and subsequently the *Georg Ots* was chartered to Tallink. ESCO increased their hold in Tallink further in 1992-1993, when first the *Tallink* was moved under the Estonian flag

and later Palkkiyhtymä sold their share in both Tallink (the company) and *Tallink* (the ship) to ESCO. By this time the Tallink fleet had grown to three ships, with the charter of Irish Ferries' *Saint Patrick II* (7,984 gross tons, 1,612 passengers, 450 cabin berths and 300 cars) during the winter seasons 1992-1995.

AN ESTONIAN JOINT VENTURE

Another major operator on the Helsinki-Tallinn route was the Tallinn-based Inreko, trading under the name Estonian New Line. Inreko had for some time been in negotiations concerning a joint service with Rederi Ab Eckerö but in spring 1993 the idea was born for an all-Estonian joint service, combining Tallink/ESCO's and Estonian New Line/Inreko's fleets. From the beginning of 1994 ESCO and Inreko established a joint subsidiary, AS Eminre, that took over the marketing name Tallink, ESCO's *Tallink*, *Georg Ots* and *Saint Patrick II*, as well as Inreko's traditional ferry *Corbière* (originally the Finland-Sweden ferry *Viking 2*) and the hydrofoils *Liisa*, *Laura* and *Jaanika*. The shunned Rederi Ab Eckerö would go on to establish their own Helsinki-Tallinn ferry service in 1994.

In May 1994, additional ferries joined Tallink service: Inreko acquired the *Vana Tallinn* (originally the England-Denmark ferry *Dana Regina*) for the Helsinki-Tallinn line, white the *Balanga Queen* (ex *Freeport*) was chartered for a new Tallinn-Travemünde (Germany) service. The *Vana Tallinn* was 10,002 gross tons, with a passenger capacity of 1,500, 858 cabin berths and 300 cars.

Disaster struck the Baltic Sea ferry services in 1994, when the Estline ferry *Estonia* sank. Estline had been established some years earlier as a joint service between ESCO and Nordström & Thulin of Sweden. However, the *Estonia* disaster did not have a long-term effect in growth of passenger numbers on the Helsinki-Tallinn line.

RE-ORGANISATION

Like many such partnerships, ESCO and Inreko's working union did not proceed quite as had been intended. From the beginning of 1995, AS Eminre was divided in two: The Helsinki-Tallinn route passed to AS Hansatee, owned by ESCO (45 per cent), Eesti Ühispank (42.50 per cent) and Inreko (12.50 per cent). The Tallinn-Travemünde line passed to an Inreko-controlled company but was closed down within months. The Inreko-owned ferries and hydrofoils continued, for the time being, sailing between Tallinn and Helsinki as before, still under the Tallink brand. The charters of the *Saint Patrick II* and *Corbière* ended in early 1995, after which the Tallink fleet consisted of the *Tallink* and *Georg Ots* of ESCO, the *Vana Tallinn* of Inreko, and during the summer months the Inreko hydrofoils *Liisa* and *Laura*.

While Tallink had the largest fleet on the Helsinki-Tallinn line, the company was not yet on a sound financial basis and both

Tallink acquired its first ferry in 1989, the former *Svea Regina* and renamed her the *Tallink*. She inaugurated a new car/passenger service between Helsinki and Tallinn. *(K Brzoza)*

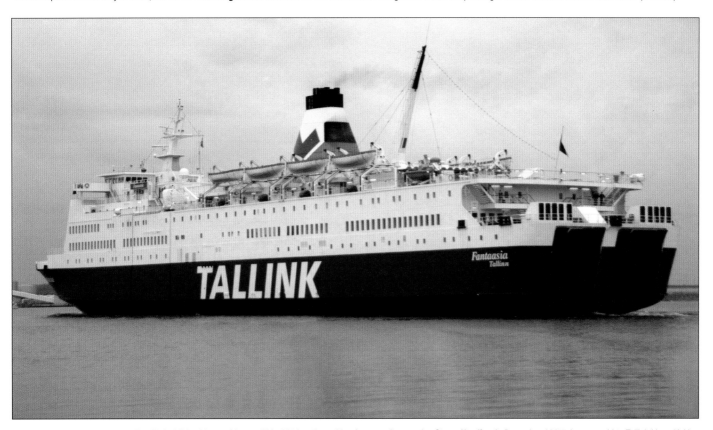

The *Fantaasia* was built as the *Turella* for Viking Line and later sold in 1988 to Stena Line for operations as the *Stena Nordica*. In December 1997 she was sold to Tallink Line. *(Jukka Huotari)*

This view at Tallinn shows the **Georg Ots** and **Vana Tallin** (ex **Dana Regina**). The **Dana Regina** was built for DFDS for their Esbjerg-Harwich service in 1974. *(Jukka Huotari)*

The distinctive-looking **Meloodia** was built originally as the **Diana II** for Viking Line in 1979. She could accommodate 1,500 passengers and 480 cars. *(Jukka Huotari)*

Eesti Ühispank and Inreko were looking to sell their shares. ESCO was interested in buying but the company was in the middle of privatisation and the Estonian Privatisation Agency prevented them from increasing their share. In the end ESCO decided instead to sell their entire share. Also interested in buying were the established large players of the northern Baltic Sea, Silja Line and Viking Line. Silja lacked the necessary funds while Viking's attempt at purchase was foiled by the Finnish Seamen's Union, who informed Viking they would insist on the Tallink ships being moved under the Finnish flag if Viking Line acquired them.

A solution for Hansatee's ownership arrived instead in the form of one man, Enn Pant. Pant was friends with Ain Hanschmidt of Eesti Ühispank and the pair engineered a new financing scheme for Tallink. As a part of this Pant acquired 44 per cent of Hansatee, while several Ühispank-related companies and Hanschmidt himself became minor shareholders. Pant became Hansatee's CEO and began a programme to improve profitability.

In autumn 1996, Hansatee chartered a new larger ship for Tallink service in the form of the *Meloodia* (originally the Finland-Sweden ferry *Diana II*). At 17,955 gross tons she was by some margin Tallink's largest ship with a passenger capacity of 1,500, cabin berths for 826 and 480 cars. In December of the same year, the *Tallink* was withdrawn from service as she did not fulfil the latest Safety of Life at Sea (SOLAS) regulations. Also in late 1996, a final rift developed between Hansatee and Inreko. Inreko sold their Hansatee shares and withdrew their ships from Tallink traffic. The hydrofoils were now operated under the brand of Linda Line, while the *Vana Tallinn* sailed for TH Ferries; both companies operated between Helsinki and Tallinn in competition with Hansatee/Tallink.

EXPANSION

For the 1997 summer season the *Meloodia* and *Georg Ots* were joined in Tallink service by the *Normandy*, (17,043 gross tons, 2,100 passengers, 1,156 cabin berths, 450 cars) that had hitherto sailed for Stena Line in the English Channel as the *Stena Normandy*. To replace the lost hydrofoils, Hansatee acquired the 1989-built fast catamaran *Tallink Express I* (430 gross tons, 250 passengers). The latter was the first ship actually purchased by Tallink since the Enn Pant takeover while the *Normandy* was returned to her owners Rederi AB Gotland in late 1997. She was replaced in the Tallink fleet by none other than the *Vana Tallinn* that was again chartered by Hansatee in January 1998. A month later a new ship joined the Tallink fleet in the form of the *Fantaasia* (16,405 gross tons, 1,700 passengers, 826 cabin berths, 425 cars). This was a reunion of sorts, as the *Fantaasia* had been the running mate of the *Meloodia* when the ships were sailing for Viking Line as the *Turella* and *Diana II*. From the beginning of 1998, Tallink introduced a new blue-red livery and funnel symbol on their ships.

In April 1999 the first car-carrying fast catamaran was introduced in the form of the *Tallink AutoExpress* (4,859 gross tons, 536 passengers, 150 cars). Tallink's smallest – yet newest – traditional ferry *Georg Ots* was withdrawn on Christmas Eve

The former Sealink vessel **Darnia** seen here as the **Neptunia** with the **Georg Ots** at Helsinki during 1999. *(Jukka Huotari)*

Tallink chartered from Irish Continental Line the **Saint Patrick II**. The Irish Ferries' vessel is seen here swinging off the berth at Helsinki in 1993. *(Rami Wirrankoski)*

The **Vana Tallinn** in full white livery outward bound from Helsinki to Estonia. *(K Brzoza)*

2000. In June 2001, a second car-carrying fast cat was introduced under the name *Tallink AutoExpress 2* (5,419 gross tons, 700 passengers, 170 cars) and at the same time the *Tallink Express I* was sold.

In the beginning of 2001 Hansatee took over the Stockholm-Tallinn service of Estline alongside the two ferries on the route, the *Regina Baltica* and *Baltic Kristina* (originally the Finland-Sweden ferries *Viking Song* and *Bore I* respectively), which were taken under charter. This was not in fact the first time Tallink had sailed to Sweden as the company had maintained a freight service between Paldiski and Kapellskär with the *Kapella* (initially named *Marine Evangeline*) since 1997. Following the takeover of Estline the *Regina Baltica* remained on the Stockholm-Tallinn route while the *Baltic Kristina* moved to the Paldiski-Kapellskär line.

NEW BUILDINGS

Hansatee had ordered their first new building, a 40,803 gross tons, 2,500-passenger cruise ferry for the Helsinki-Tallinn route, from Aker Finnyards in Rauma in August 2000. The ship was delivered in May 2002 as the *Romantika* and placed on 22-hour cruise service between Helsinki and Tallinn. The *Romantika* was essentially a developed version of Viking Line's *Cinderella* of 1989 – which also sailed on the same route – and as such she was perfectly suited for the service she sailed on.

Also during 2002 Hansatee changed their name to Tallink Grupp, finally putting to rest the double identity of Hansatee and Tallink. Within the year Tallink Grupp acquired both the *Meloodia* and *Regina Baltica* from ESCO. The charter of the *Baltic Kristina*, however, was allowed to lapse. With the arrival of the *Romantika*, the *Fantaasia* and *Vana Tallinn* left the Helsinki-Tallinn link; the former moved to the Stockholm-Tallinn line as the *Regina Baltica*'s running mate, while the *Vana Tallinn* went to the Paldiski-Kapellskär route.

A sister ship to the *Romantika* was ordered in late 2002 and arrived in March 2004 as the *Victoria I*. The new ship was given a larger cabin capacity (2,252 versus 2,172) and placed on the Stockholm-Tallinn route, replacing the *Fantaasia*. The latter was, in turn, placed on a new Helsinki-Tallinn-St Petersburg service. This was not a success and the route was closed down after less than a year of service.

May 2004 saw Estonia join the EU, which also signalled the end of tax-free sales on the Helsinki-Tallinn service. While other operators were convinced this would decrease passenger numbers and therefore downsized their fleets, Tallink's leadership saw the change – correctly – as a chance for further growth, as cheaper prices in Estonia would continue to attract large numbers of Finnish passengers. As a result of this, in addition to the *Victoria I*, no fewer than three other ships joined the Tallink fleet in 2004: the fast monohull ferries *Tallink AutoExpress 3* and *Tallink AutoExpress 4* were purchased for the Helsinki-Tallinn line, while the freighter *Regal Star* was acquired for the Paldiski-Kapellskär route. The latter's acquisition allowed the *Kapella* to switch to the Helsinki-Tallinn line.

In late 2004 Tallink placed an order for yet another new building, an enlarged version of the *Romantika* for the Helsinki-Tallinn line, to be delivered in 2006; this ship was eventually

named the *Galaxy*. In 2005, three more new-building orders were placed: Aker Finnyards in Helsinki was to build a sister ship to the under-construction *Galaxy* as well as a fast conventional ferry based on the *SeaFrance Rodin* of 2001. Fincantieri in Italy were to build a further fast conventional ferry, this one based on the *Moby Wonder* of 2001. All three new-building orders also included options for sister ships although only one of these was taken up.

BALTIC SUPERFASTS

The Greek-based Superfast Ferries had, since 2001, operated a duo (later a trio) of fast ro-pax ferries between Finland and Germany. Although the route was successful, Superfast were interested in selling; Tallink, meanwhile, had ambitions for a service to Germany and were interested in buying. In April 2006 Tallink purchased Superfast Ferries' Hanko-Rostock route and the *Superfast VII*, *Superfast VIII* and *Superfast IX*, (all 30,285 gross tons, 626 passengers and 661 cars, 1,920 lane metres of freight) alongside the temporary right to use the Superfast name, for 310 million Euros. Soon afterwards the Superfasts were repainted with 'Superfast operated by Tallink' logos and moved under the Estonian flag. An intermediate call at Paldiski was added on the route but this proved a mistake and was discontinued after only two months.

Just a month after the Superfasts had been acquired, Tallink took delivery of the new *Galaxy* (48,915 gross tons, 2,800 passengers, 2,500 cabin berths, 420 cars, 1,130 lane metres of freight). The ship made impression with her unusual livery – designed by the Estonian artist Navitrolla, a personal friend of Enn Pant. She was placed on the Helsinki-Tallinn run in place of the *Romantika*. The *Romantika* in turn replaced the *Regina Baltica* which moved to a new Stockholm-Riga service that had been opened a month before with the *Fantaasia*. There was no need for two ships on the latter service and thus the *Fantaasia* was chartered out and eventually sold.

Meanwhile, the famous Finnish ferry operator Silja Line had been placed for sale by its owners Sea Containers. Tallink was one of the companies to submit a bid and this was accepted by Sea Containers in June 2006. In July, Tallink took over Silja Line's Finland-Sweden services and the six ferries sailing on them (*Silja Serenade*, *Silja Symphony*, *Silja Europa*, *Silja Festival*, *Sea Wind* and *Sky Wind*). Essentially, Tallink had doubled the size of their fleet in 2006 and taken over one of the best-known ferry brands in the world.

TALLINK SILJA LINE

Unfortunately for Tallink, their takeover of Silja Line was negatively perceived by a large section of both the Finnish and Swedish populations. Matters were not helped by the fact that in Sweden, the two brands were turned into a single brand, Tallink Silja Line. More damaging to Tallink's reputation were reports in the yellow papers of the Tallink leadership's allegedly egregious behaviour and mistreatment of the crew on board the *Silja Symphony* in October 2006. This incident set the tone for media treatment of Tallink as misbehaving upstarts out to destroy the valued Silja Line brand, which continues to this day in Finnish and Swedish media.

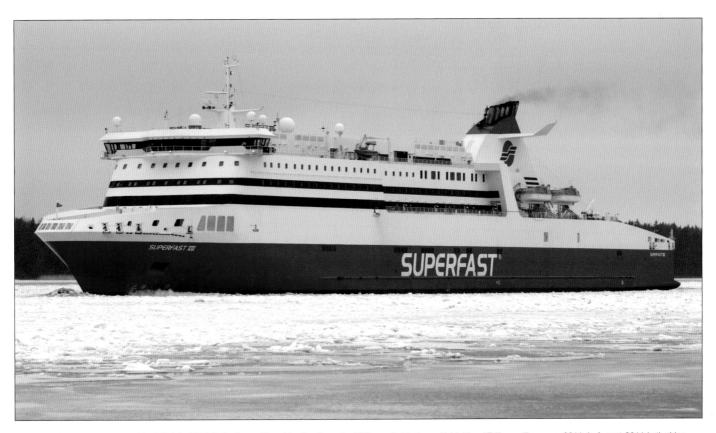

The **Superfast VIII** was acquired by Tallink in 2006. Both she and her sister the **Superfast VII** operated between Helsinki and Tallinn until summer 2011. In August 2011 both ships were chartered by the Estonian company to Stena Line for use on their service between Cairnryan and Belfast. *(K Brzoza)*

This view shows the Finnish-built **Galaxy** outward bound from Mariehamn (Aland) with the **Silja Europa** also leaving in the backgound for Sweden. *(Miles Cowsill)*

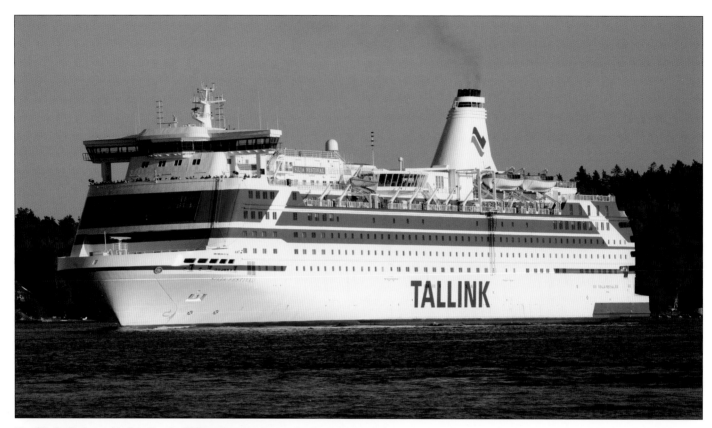

The **Silja Festival** was originally built as the **Wellamo** for service between Sweden and Finland. With the takeover of Silja Line by Tallink the vessel was transferred to the Stockholm-Riga route and currently operates under the Tallink brand. *(Miles Cowsill)*

The much-travelled **Regina Baltica** is seen here leaving Stockholm for Riga in 2008. The vessel was originally built as the **Viking Song** in 1980. *(Miles Cowsill)*

TRANSFORMATION

The first immediate change to take place after the 2006 acquisitions was the move of the three Superfasts to a new Tallinn-Helsinki-Rostock service from the beginning of 2007. This allowed them to sail both between Finland and Germany as well as provide day cruises from Helsinki to Tallinn.

In April 2007 Tallink took delivery of their first new built fast ro-pax ferry for the Helsinki-Tallinn line, the *Star* from Aker Finnyards (36,249 gross tons, 1,900 passengers, 520 cabin berths, 450 cars, 1981 lane metres of cargo). One year later Tallink took delivery of the *Star*'s running mate *Superstar* (36,277 gross tons, 2,020 passengers, 1,256 cabin berths, 665 cars, 1,930 lane metres). These two ships, capable of making the crossing between Helsinki and Tallinn in only two hours, transformed the route and replaced no fewer than five older vessels: the *Meloodia*, *Tallink AutoExpress*, *Tallink AutoExpress 2*, *Tallink AutoExpress 3* and *Tallink AutoExpress 4* were all sold.

The day cruises provided between Helsinki and Tallinn by the three Superfasts ended in October 2008 when the Helsinki terminal of all ships sailing to Germany was moved to the new Vuosaari freight harbour. From now on the Superfasts only sailed between Helsinki and Rostock. The Finland-Germany service proved less profitable than had been initially anticipated and coinciding with the change of harbour, the *Superfast IX* was chartered out to Marine Atlantic in Canada.

LATEST SHIPS

In July 2008 Tallink took delivery of their last new building for the Helsinki-Tallinn line to date, when the *Galaxy*'s sister ship *Baltic Princess* was delivered. The younger sister is essentially identical to the *Galaxy*, but fitted with more powerful engines, capable of a 24-knot service speed instead of 22 knots. The *Baltic Princess* replaced the *Galaxy* on the 22-hour cruise service from Helsinki while she, in turn, moved to Silja Line's Turku-Stockholm service, replacing the *Silja Festival*, which moved to Tallink's Stockholm-Riga service. She replaced the *Vana Tallinn* which had sailed on the route since April 2007 and which was finally, moved to the Paldiski-Kapellskär service until 2009. She was sold in 2011.

A third *Galaxy*-class ship arrived in April 2009 as the *Baltic Queen*. Identical to the *Baltic Princess* except in terms of her livery, the *Baltic Queen* was placed on the Tallinn-Stockholm line where she replaced the *Romantika*. The *Romantika*, in turn, moved to the Riga-Stockholm line, replacing the *Regina Baltica*. The latter remains under Tallink ownership to this day but has spent her time since 2009 under charter to various different operators.

GERMAN SERVICE ENDS

The acquisition of Superfast Ferries' Finland-Germany services had proven to be a mistake on the part of Tallink. Finnlines, the other operator on the routes, had taken delivery of five new, large and fast ro-pax ferries for the route soon after Tallink's purchase of the Superfasts and hence drastically altered the balance on the routes. In autumn 2009 Tallink's Helsinki-Rostock service

An impressive view of the colourful **Galaxy** inward bound to Stockholm. The vessel was bulilt by AKER Yards at Rauma, Finland and can accommodate some 2,800 passengers and 300 cars. *(Miles Cowsill)*

The **Baltic Princess** is seen here outward bound from Tallinn for Helsinki prior to her transfer to the Stockholm-Turku service in 2013. *(Miles Cowsill)*

Possibly one of the best appointed ships on the Helsinki-Tallinn route is Tallink's **Star**. The Finnish-built ship leaves Helsinki on her late afternoon run to Estonia in March 2013. *(Miles Cowsill)*

The **Romantika** leaves Stockholm for Tallinn on her overnight service to Estonia. In May 2009 she was transferred to the Riga route. *(Miles Cowsill)*

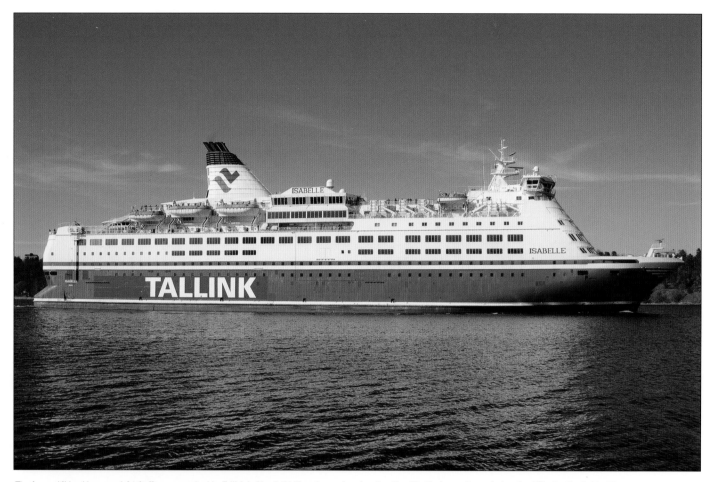

The former Viking Line vessel *Isabella* was acquired by Tallink in March 2013 and was placed on the Riga-Stockholm service replacing the *Silja Festival*. *(Kim Viktor)*

changed to a seasonal one, to which Finnlines answered by opening a Rostock service of their own. In summer 2011 Stena Line offered to take the *Superfast VII* and *VIII* under charter for three years, to which Tallink readily agreed. The Helsinki-Rostock service was then closed in August 2011.

In response to the arrival of Viking Line's new cruise ferry *Viking Grace* on the Turku-Stockholm line, Tallink decided to re-organise their own fleet. The *Baltic Princess* moved under the Silja Line brand to sail on the Turku-Stockholm route, replacing the *Silja Europa*, which in turn took over the 22-hour cruise service from Helsinki to Tallinn. A factor in this change was the *Silja Europa*'s unreliable engines which had proven problematic on the high-intensity Turku-Stockholm route.

A further effect of the arrival of the *Viking Grace* was the sale of Viking Line's *Isabella* to Tallink. Viking Line had intended to sell the ship once the *Viking Grace* entered service but when no buyer was found they intended to switch her to the Helsinki-Tallinn route. Tallink, meanwhile, wished to avoid this. A solution benefiting both parties was found when Tallink purchased the *Isabella* in April 2013. Renamed *Isabelle*, the ship was placed on the Riga-Stockholm service, replacing the *Silja Festival*.

At the time of writing, Tallink's fleet consists of the following ships: *Silja Europa*, *Star* and *Superstar* on the Helsinki-Tallinn

line, *Baltic Queen* and *Victoria I* on the Tallinn-Stockholm service, *Romantika* and *Isabelle* on the Riga-Stockholm link, *Regal Star* on the Paldiski-Kapellskär cargo route and *Sea Wind* on the Turku-Stockholm cargo crossing. Operated under the Silja Line brand are the *Silja Serenade* and *Silja Symphony* on the Helsinki-Stockholm route alongside the *Galaxy* and *Baltic Princess* on the Turku-Stockholm route. Owned by Tallink but chartered out are the *Regina Baltica*, *Stena Superfast VII*, *Stena Superfast VIII* and *Atlantic Vision*, while the *Silja Festival* is laid up in Riga. The ships of Silja Line and Tallink make the company the third-largest ferry operator in the world in terms of gross tonnage and the largest in the world in terms of passenger berths.

Ferry Publications will be publishing in December 2013 a history of Silja Line written by Kalle Id. The book also traces the development and history of Tallink who subsequently acquired Silja Line. For further information on this book visit ferrypublications.co.uk.

2 Norwegian Breakaway
by John Hendy

The Miami-based Norwegian Cruise Line (now abbreviated to Norwegian, rather than NCL) is an innovator in cruise travel with a 46-year history of breaking the boundaries of traditional cruising. The company introduced what they have termed 'Freestyle Cruising' which has drastically changed the industry to suit the American market by giving guests more freedom and flexibility.

Today, Norwegian invites guests to "Cruise Like a Norwegian" on one of 12 purpose-built 'Freestyle Cruising' ships, providing them with the opportunity to enjoy a relaxed, resort-style cruise holiday on some of the newest and most contemporary ships at sea. Recently, the line was named 'Europe's Leading Cruise Line' by the World Travel Awards for the fifth consecutive year. During 2013, four of the company's vessels were based in Europe: the *Norwegian Epic* in the western Mediterranean, the *Norwegian Jade* in the Adriatic and Greek Islands, the *Norwegian Spirit* in the Mediterranean and the *Norwegian Star* in the Baltic.

Although not to everyone's taste, Norwegian's largest ship, the one-off 'F-3' class 4,100-passenger *Norwegian Epic* has been named 'Best Overall Cruise Ship' by the readers of Travel Weekly two years in a row and 'Best Ship for Sea Days' by Cruise Critic. Yet the greatest criticism made of her is that, in spite of air retractor fans, smoke from her centrally sited Casino is allowed to

permeate throughout the atrium and nearby restaurants, a problem that has not been altogether solved in the 'Breakaway'. For the British market this state of affairs would now be largely unacceptable.

Following the successful launch of the partially redesigned 155,873 gross ton 'Epic' on 25th October 2010, the company announced that it had reached an agreement with Meyer Werft of Papenburg, Germany to build two new next generation 'Freestyle Cruising' ships for delivery in spring 2013 and spring 2014. This followed an acrimonious dispute with STX Europe after the cancellation of a second 'Epic' and an option for a third vessel at the start of the global economic downturn. Changes to the original design, after the sale of 50 per cent of Norwegian Cruise Lines to Apollo Management in 2007, inevitably meant higher overall costs for what was then the World's third largest cruise ship.

Under the controlling hand of Kevin Sheehan, Norwegian's Chief Executive Officer, significant changes have occurred since 2008 and it is widely accepted that his driving force has lifted Norwegian out of the doldrums. The company has made great efforts to improve its relationships with the travel agent fraternity via its 'Partners First' initiative while passenger satisfaction has been given priority. The business went public in January 2013

The construction of the **Norwegian Breakaway** is well advanced inside Meyer Werft's impressive building dock II at Papenburg. *(Meyer Werft)*

This trials picture of the **Norwegian Breakaway** illustrates the vessel's impressive outside recreational area and Aqua Park surrounding the funnel. *(Meyer Werft)*

En route for New York, the vessel was at Southampton on 29th April 2013 and is seen passing Calshot Spit. *(Darren Holdaway)*

since when its shares have risen by an impressive 60 per cent.

The 'Breakaway' is the first ship to be delivered with Sheehan in control of the company and is therefore the first to embrace his personal cruising philosophy. He believed from the outset that it was vital that guests were made aware that they were at sea as on so many resort ships of this size, this is all too easy to forget. Sheehan sees the ship as a significant industry statement; "We have always been focused on a disciplined approach to capacity growth. Our decision to add two new ships reflects the significant progress we have made in improving our operating performance and repositioning the Company over the last several years. Building on the success and popularity of the *Norwegian Epic*, we are taking the best of what she has to offer, as well as drawing on our legacy of innovation in the cruise industry, in creating a new class of 'Freestyle Cruising' vessel that is sure to provide our guests with the unparalleled freedom and flexibility they have come to expect on a Norwegian cruise."

'FREESTYLE CRUISING'

Norwegian pioneered the concept of 'Freestyle Cruising' offering guests the freedom and flexibility to enjoy their cruise holiday on their own terms, including multiple dining venues, no set times or seating arrangements for meals, relaxed attire, a variety of accommodation and world-class entertainment. The Company took this concept to the next level with the introduction of the St Nazaire-built *Norwegian Epic* in June 2010. The 4,100-passenger vessel was named the "entertainment ship" with a variety of shows and venues that equal, if not better, land-based resorts such as those found in Las Vegas.

The *Norwegian Breakaway*'s features include hull art by New York artist Peter Max, seafood restaurant Ocean Blue by Chef Geoffrey Zakarian, bakery by Buddy Valastro and fitness classes and a display from the ship's godmothers, the Rockettes (an American precision dance company).

Both new vessels, the largest passenger/cruise ships to be built in Germany, are fitted with approximately 4,000 passenger berths and a rich cabin mix. The contract price for the two vessels was approximately 1.2 billion Euros. Papenburg-based Meyer Werft had previously delivered Norwegian's four 'Jewel' class ships; *Norwegian Gem* in 2007, *Norwegian Pearl* and *Norwegian Jade* in 2006, and *Norwegian Jewel* in 2005. The two new vessels are the eighth and ninth that the Company have built with Meyer Werft.

CONSTRUCTION

On 22nd September 2011 the first piece of steel was cut at Meyer Werft for the construction of the *Norwegian Breakaway* that was set for delivery in April 2013. The first plate of steel took four minutes to cut by a plasma torch in the yard's state of the art facility. This became a supporting part of the double bottom in the centre of the new ship.

The keel laying of yard number S.678, was celebrated at the Papenburg shipyard on Friday 4th May 2012 when the first of 73 blocks of the vessel was lifted into the covered building dock II. Kevin Sheehan laid the traditional 'lucky coin', before the block was put down by the 800-ton crane. This weighed more than 350 tons and marked the commencement of the ship's construction.

The **Norwegian Breakaway** is nudged by tugs at Meyer Werft prior to sailing down the River Ems for trials. The hull art is by Peter Max whose signature appears more prominently than the ship's name. *(Meyer Werft)*

Gaming tables in the Breakaway Casino. *(Norwegian Cruise Line)*

Computer-driven plans, graphics and tank tests achieved a far sleeker hull line than that of the *Norwegian Epic*. The 'Breakaway' can achieve the same speeds as the earlier ship with up to 20 per cent less power. Lighter steel construction has also helped the vessel to achieve significant fuel savings and every effort has been made to save on energy; this even includes the automatic switching off of lights at times when guests are not using their cabins.

The 'Breakaway' class ships, *Norwegian Breakaway* and *Norwegian Getaway*, are each 144,017 gross tons and have approximately 4,000 passenger berths. These ships represent an opportunity for the Norwegian guest to 'break away' from the routine of work, school, and daily stress, and find a true respite at sea. The new vessels effectively draw upon the best features from all of Norwegian's existing ships, based on the line's experience of having launched ten ships in the past ten years – starting with the *Norwegian Star* and *Norwegian Sun* in 2001 and culminating with the launch of the *Norwegian Epic* in 2010.

The Prime Meridian Bar is sited at the after end of Deck 8. *(Norwegian Cruise Line)*

The comfortable Savor Restaurant, with its eye catching carpets and overhead lighting, serves traditional cuisine and is situated aft on Deck 6. *(Norwegian Cruise Line)*

The Raw Bar, highlighting crustaceans and wines by the glass, is situated midships on Deck 8. *(Norwegian Cruise Line)*

A two-bedroom/ two bathroom Haven Family Villa. Some 42 suites are provided on Decks 15 and 16 and are serviced by their own restaurant and cocktail bar. *(Norwegian Cruise Line)*

Located next to the Casino, Bar 21 features video poker and multiple plasma television screens. *(Norwegian Cruise Line)*

The Humidor Cigar Lounge is perhaps the most traditional space within the ship. *(Norwegian Cruise Line)*

The ships' names were chosen from 230,000 entries received in "Norwegian's Cruising for Names" contest held in conjunction with national newspaper USA Today. Their staterooms combine the form and function of the line's 'Jewel' class ships with the modern and contemporary design touches of the *Norwegian Epic*. A rich mix of stateroom options are available including the innovative Studios, designed and priced for solo travellers, the re-introduction of Oceanview staterooms, Balcony and Mini-Suites, along with Spa Balcony, Mini-Suites and Suites in close proximity to the spa. The ships also feature The Haven by Norwegian, comprised of 42 suites at the top of the ship and 18 additional suites located throughout the ship.

Following a series of extensive tests and machinery trials, on Tuesday 26th February 2013, the *Norwegian Breakaway* was floated out of Meyer Werft's building dock II after an amazingly brief building period of just 17 months. The float-out commenced at around 07.00 after which the ship was berthed alongside the yard's outfitting pier. At the fitting-out berth, the remaining work, tests and trials were carried out and within the week, the first crew-members moved into their cabins on board and familiarised themselves with the ship itself and its numerous systems.

INNOVATIVE DESIGN

The ship's architects are the Swedish company Tillberg Design in conjunction with SMC Design of London. The vessel combines innovative design including twin key elements which serve to make this ship different from her fleet companions. These are The Waterfront and 678 Ocean Place with three unique decks of dining, entertainment and more, along with the largest aqua park and the largest ropes course at sea, and the first ever salt room in the luxurious spa.

The new concept includes an oceanfront boardwalk lined with shops, restaurants and bars, combined with three decks of dining, bars, entertainment, gaming and more. "With our newest ship we are continuing our tradition of innovation with a brand new ship design that will provide our guests with a unique experience unlike anything else at sea," said Kevin Sheehan. Guests are able to enjoy al fresco dining while also admiring the sea which is fine in calm weather but which might possibly deliver adverse consequences during a gale. Located on Deck 8, The Waterfront is a revolutionary outdoor feature that adds a whole new dimension to the line's signature 'Freestyle Cruising', by offering a number of seaside venues that feature sea views.

The hub of the ship is 678 Ocean Place, a space that connects three decks of daytime and night-time amusements. There are a total of 17 dining venues combined on both 678 Ocean Place and The Waterfront, along with 12 bars and lounges. Norwegian also introduce a new dining concept called Ocean Blue, the line's first ever all-seafood restaurant, which includes a premium raw bar, along with a separate sushi bar.

The Waterfront

The Waterfront features eight outdoor dining and lounging options, including signature Norwegian favourites like Moderno Churrascaria, Cagney's Steakhouse, La Cucina, Shaker's Cocktail Bar, Malting's Beer & Whiskey Bar and the newest addition,

The comfortable and relaxing Shakers Cocktail Bar is on Deck 8. *(Norwegian Cruise Line)*

The Taste Restaurant is one of 17 dining venues and is situated adjacent to the Savor Restaurant. *(Norwegian Cruise Line)*

The ship's hub is 678 Ocean Place - an atrium that links three decks. *(Norwegian Cruise Line)*

Ocean Blue on The Waterfront, with outdoor seating and a special takeaway menu. The Waterfront will also feature another first for Norwegian – a gelato bar serving a selection of flavours.

678 Ocean Place

On Deck 8, 678 Ocean Place connects The Waterfront outdoor spaces with interior dining venues for Moderno; Cagney's; Shaker's; La Cucina; Malting's and Ocean Blue, including the raw and sushi bars. An elegant modern take on an ocean-inspired theme, Ocean Blue is the newest addition to Norwegian's Freestyle Dining line-up and features a premium raw bar and a sushi bar.

"In a recent guest survey, our guests chose a seafood restaurant as the number one type of restaurant they would like on board our ships," said Sheehan. "We listened to that feedback when planning the dining on the *Norwegian Breakaway* and have launched Ocean Blue as our newest signature restaurant concept."

La Cucina celebrates the Tuscan countryside and will continue to serve Norwegian's Italian dishes to guests who choose to dine either al fresco on the outdoor patio on The Waterfront, in the main restaurant or in the interior terrace option, giving them the opportunity to dine along the interior walkway beneath traditional-style lanterns, mock wooden beams and greenery.

Along with her new design, this luxury cruise ship offers guests a number of special features and comfort: approximately 75 per cent of the staterooms are outside staterooms, most of them with their own balconies. The ship also includes staterooms designed and priced for single travellers, continuing the tradition that began on the *Norwegian Epic*, along with The Haven by Norwegian, a top-of-the-ship complex that offers guests a range of suites, a private restaurant, lounge, covered pool area and sun deck.

"We set out to deliver a ship that would really stand apart and our collaboration with the Norwegian team has been outstanding," said Bernard Meyer, managing partner with Meyer Werft. "It's quite an accomplishment to build a vessel of this size and calibre in just 18 months."

The latest engine technology, the diesel-electric Azipod XO pod drive system (rather than the shaft system used in the *Norwegian Epic*), improved hydrodynamics as well as effective energy saving, heat recovery or ballast water treatment guarantee at significantly reduced operating costs. In addition, the ship was designed according to the latest security regulations. The building of the *Norwegian Breakaway* was supported by the Federal Ministry of Economics and Technology and the federal state of Lower Saxony with an aid for innovation for a ship-type design and the first use of innovative components.

Extensive tests and trials of all systems and intensive training of the crew kept everyone busy in the last weeks prior to her 25th April delivery in Bremerhaven. The ship has an overall length of 324m, and is 39.7m wide. Her construction complies with the latest safety standards and she meets all valid environmental regulations.

Following her handover, the 'Breakaway' left Germany for Rotterdam from where she cruised to Southampton. After being inspected by the travel press she commenced her maiden trans-Atlantic crossing from Southampton to New York, where her naming ceremony took place.

Known as New York's ship, the 'Breakaway' is the largest vessel to be based at the city's Manhattan Cruise Terminal throughout the year, sailing to King's Wharf at Bermuda for the summer on seven-night breaks as from 12th May 2013. From 6th October 2013 until April 2014, the ship is engaged on both 7 and 12 night cruises to the Bahamas, Florida and the southern Caribbean. Sister ship, the *Norwegian Getaway* is expected to appear in Miami on 1st February 2014.

'BREAKAWAY PLUS'

In July 2013 Norwegian Cruise Line announced that it had confirmed an order for a second 'Breakaway Plus' cruise ship with Meyer Werft for delivery in spring 2017. Along with the first 'Breakaway Plus' ship, which is scheduled for delivery in October 2015, these two new vessels will be the largest in the line's fleet at approximately 163,000 gross tons and 4,200 passenger berths each and will be similar in design and innovation to the 'Breakaway' class.

The combined contract cost of the two 'Breakaway Plus' class ships is approximately 1.4 billion Euros. The company has export credit financing in place that provides financing for 80 per cent of the contract price. With further new elements, yet to be announced, and an additional deck to incorporate extra innovations, the two 'Breakaway Plus' ships will offer even more ways to experience all that the revitalised Norwegian has to offer.

Norwegian Breakaway Fact File:

Gross tonnage	144,017
Length overall	324m
Moulded breadth	39.7m
Number of decks	18
Draught	8.3m
Engine output	62,400kW in total
Propulsion power	35,000kW
Speed	21.5 knots
Number of passengers	4,000
Number of passenger cabins	2,014
Number of outside cabins (including suites)	1,508
Number of inside cabins	506
Crew	1,600
Number of theatre seats	770
Number of dining options	27
Total weight of applied paint	300 tons
Total length of laid cables	2,154km
Total length of laid pipes	400km
Flag	Bahamas
Classification	DNV

3 Transbordador Islas Canarias
Matt Davies looks at the ferries of the Canary Islands

The Canary Islands archipelago is located in the Atlantic Ocean off the northwest coast of Africa in the proximity of Morocco and the Western Sahara, and at the shortest point is just 60 miles across. Although part of Spain, the islands are governed autonomously from the Capital Las Palmas de Gran Canaria. There are seven main islands; from largest to smallest; Tenerife, Fuerteventura, Gran Canaria, Lanzarote, La Palma, La Gomera and El Hierro. In addition there are six small islands of which only La Graciosa, home to 600 people and located off Lanzarote, is inhabited.

Some 2.1 million people live in the islands and the majority are on Tenerife (900,000) and Gran Canaria (800,500). The other five islands are much less densely populated; Lanzarote is home to 141,000, Fuerteventura 103,000, La Palma 86,000, La Gomera 22,000 and El Hierro is home to just 11,000. Population has grown considerably and consequently there has been an explosion in both passenger and freight ferry operations over the last 20 years as demand for interisland travel and to and from the Spanish mainland has increased. The expansion has seen longstanding operator Trasmediterranea gradually retreat from interisland sailings as Norwegian-owned Lineas Fred. Olsen and the Canary Islands Company Naviera Armas have expanded considerably with modern purpose-built tonnage. Meanwhile, German-owned shipping company OPDR has been gradually eroding Trasmediterranea's freight market from the mainland with a service from Seville and since 2011 the line's weekly passenger, car and freight service to the mainland has come under heavy competition from Armas who have opened a new service to nearby Huelva. Trasmediterranea now operate just three vessels, each of which undertakes a weekly round trip to the islands – a freighter and a ro-pax operate from Cadiz and a con-ro operates from Seville.

Fred. Olsen Express has, however, stuck firmly to interisland routes since inception in 1974 when as Ferry Gomera the company started with a single vessel sailing between Tenerife and La Gomera. The company links all seven islands with a fleet of five purpose-built fast ferries and is one of only a few operators in the world to make a commercial success out of fast ferry operations. Naviera Armas, meanwhile, have been engaged in interisland cargo shipping since the 1940s. They entered ro-ro operations in the 1970s and moved into the passenger operations in 1995 when two purpose-built ro-pax vessels were introduced. In the early 2000s Armas embarked on ambitious fleet building programme, taking delivery of no fewer than seven passenger vessels between 2004 and 2011 from Vigo shipbuilder Barreras. In 2005 when

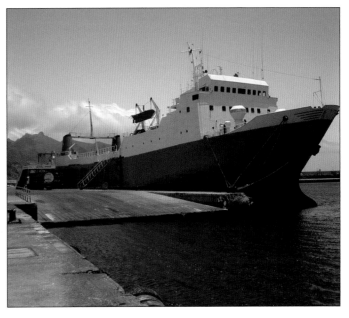

The 1979-built ro-ro freighter **Volcán de Tahiche** was one of eight sister vessels built by ASCON in Vigo. Purchased by Armas in 1995 she was used on interisland services and on a fortnightly service to Nouakchott, Mauritania and Dakhla, Western Sahara. She was withdrawn and scrapped in Turkey in 2010 when her African service was taken over by Boluda. *(Matt Davies)*

Trasmediterranea was privatised Armas took an 8 per cent stake in a consortium with other investors, though the subsequent injection of capital by principal shareholder Acciona has now reduced Armas's holding to 4 per cent. Armas currently operate five passenger car ferries on interisland services plus a further vessel on a weekly service to and from Huelva on the mainland. In recent years the company has over expanded realising a significant surplus in tonnage. Consequently, one of the line's original ro-pax vessels has been sold, a freighter chartered out to competitor Trasmediterranea and two vessels redeployed to new services form Motril in Spain to Morocco and Melilla in North Africa.

To complete the Canaries picture, two freight operators are worthy of a brief mention. In 2011, Spanish shipping conglomerate Boluda Corporation started a new and ultimately unsuccessful weekly passenger and freight service from Seville to Gran Canaria and Tenerife using the 32 year old ro-pax *Reyes B*, at one time the P&O vessel the *European Envoy*. Boluda continues to operate a weekly ro-ro service from Las Palmas to Cape Verde, Nouadhibou and Nouakchott in Mauritania. Finally, since the 1990s, OPDR Canarias has operated two or three con-ro vessels from Seville to the Islands and significantly upgraded operations in 2006 when new purpose-built tonnage was introduced.

The **Barlovento** was formerly the **Pride of Cherbourg** of P&O. Purchased by Fred. Olsen in 1994 she entered service as the **Banaderos** between Santa Cruz de Tenerife and Agaete, Gran Canaria. In 2000 she was renamed the **Barlovento** and introduced on new services from Los Cristianos to El Hierro and La Palma in direct competition with Trasmediterranea. Replaced by further fast craft in 2005, she was withdrawn and sold to SAOS ferries. *(Matt Davies)*

The 12,895 gross tons **Volcán de Taburiente** is one of Armas's smaller units. She was built to operate from Los Cristianos, to El Hierro, San Sebastián de La Gomera and Santa Cruz de La Palma and entered service in 2006 replacing the **Volcán de Teneguía**. She no longer serves the remote island of El Hierro following a reduction in subsidy payments by the Canarian government but in late 2013 the route restarted using the chartered Austal AutoExpress 79 catamaran **Alcántara Dos**. *(Matt Davies)*

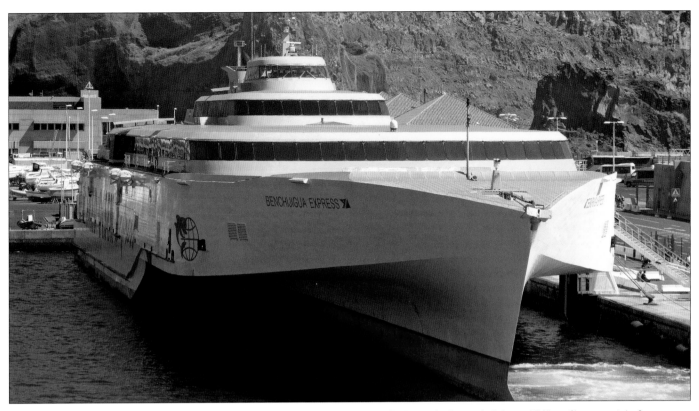

The 126-metre, 2005-built Austal Trimaran **Benchijigua Express** is operated by Fred. Olsen from Los Cristianos to La Gomera, La Palma and El Hierro. She crosses to La Gomera, where she is seen, in just 30 minutes at a speed of 40 knots and can carry 1,350 passengers and 341 cars. She is the fifth vessel on the route to carry the name 'Benchijigua' since Ferry Gomera started in 1974. *(Matt Davies)*

The 17,343 gross tons **Volcán de Tamasite** was the first of a quartet of sister vessels built for Armas between 2004 and 2007 by Barreras in Vigo. She replaced an earlier vessel of the same name on the crossing from Las Palmas de Gran Canaria to Morro Jable at the southern tip of Fuerteventura. The first pair of the quartet are day vessels without cabins and are slower at 21 knots. She is seen here departing Santa Cruz de Tenerife at daybreak. *(Matt Davies)*

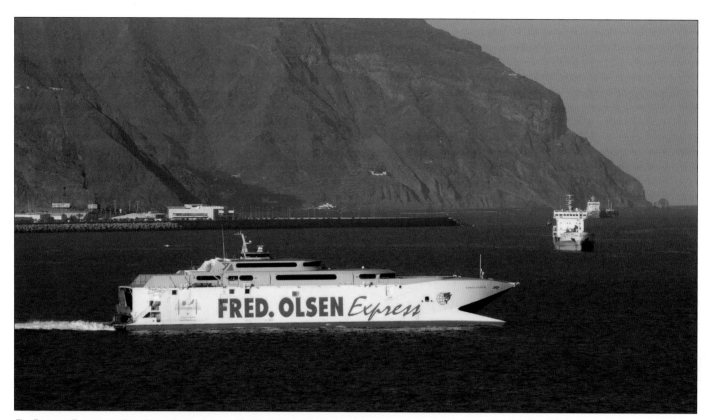

The **Bonanza Express** was Fred. Olsen's first Incat vessel. The 93-metre craft, which is seen here departing Santa Cruz de Tenerife in 2013, entered service in 1999 on the crossing between Santa Cruz de Tenerife and Agaete, Gran Canaria. In late 2012 she replaced a conventional ferry, the **Betancuria**, on the route from Las Palmas de Gran Canaria to Morro Jable and Porto Rosario on Fuerteventura and Arrecife, Lanzarote. *(Matt Davies)*

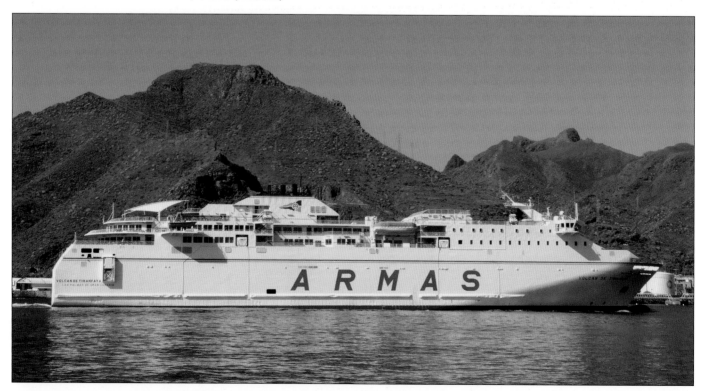

The second Armas's quartet, the **Volcán de Timanfaya**, was delivered in 2005 and is seen departing Santa Cruz de Tenerife in April 2013. The 19,976 gross ton vessel can carry 1,466 passengers and 395 cars. Along with her sisters she is employed on a complex pattern of inter-worked routes covering four sailings a day between Tenerife and Gran Canaria, daily sailings from Gran Canaria to Lanzarote and to Fuerteventura and a weekly sailing from Tenerife to El Hierro. In 2011 she launched Armas's first service from Motril to Melilla, returning to the interisland service in 2012. *(Matt Davies)*

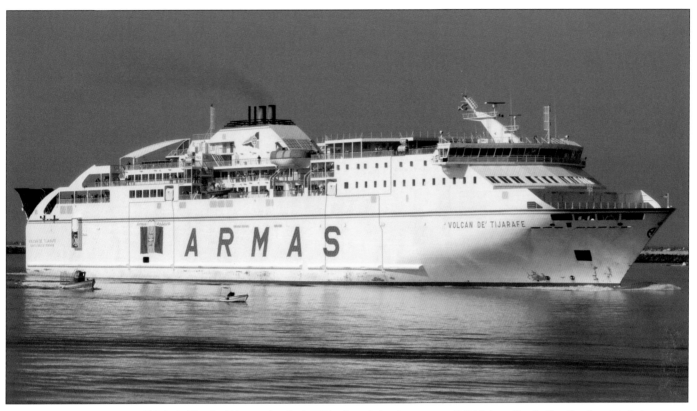

Final vessel of Armas's quartet is the **Volcán de Tijarafe** which entered service in 2007 and was deployed on a new weekly link between Tenerife, Gran Canaria and the Portuguese island of Madeira which was extended to Portimao on the Portuguese mainland from 2008. In 2011 she returned to inter-island traffic being replaced on the route by the larger new building ferry the **Volcán de Tinamar**. *(Matt Davies)*

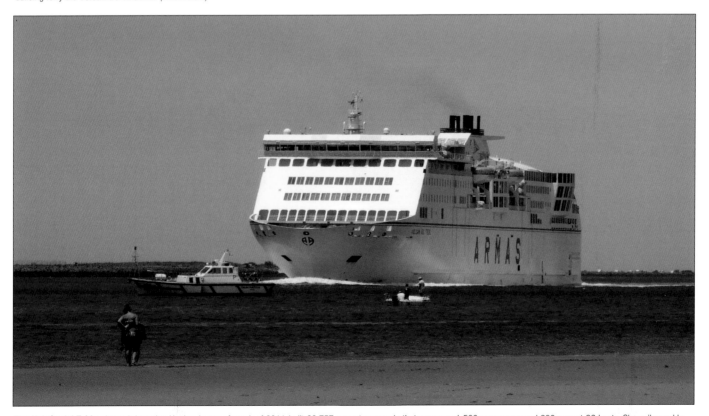

The **Volcán del Teide**, pictured departing Huelva, is one of a pair of 2011-built 29,757 gross ton vessels that can carry 1,500 passengers and 600 cars at 26 knots. She sails weekly from Tenerife to Huelva via Gran Canaria, crossing from the latter in 36 hours. Her sister the **Volcán de Tinamar** spent her first season sailing on the Canaries-Madeira-Portimao route and now operates between Motril and Melilla. *(Matt Davies)*

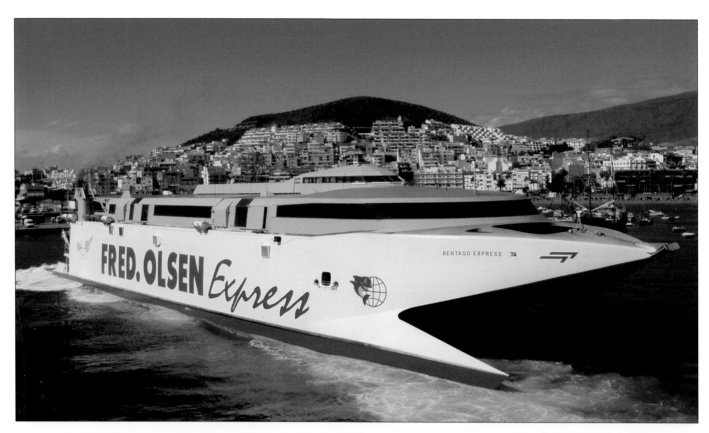

Fred. Olsen operate two 98-metre Incat craft; the **Bencomo Express** of 1999 and the **Bentago Express** of 2000 which is seen departing Los Cristianos. The vessels which started life as the **Benchijigua Express** and **Bentayga Express** now operate on the 90-minute crossing between Santa Cruz de Tenerife and Agaete, Gran Canaria route. *(Matt Davies)*

In 1980 Fred. Olsen commenced sailings between Playa Blanca, Lanzarote and Corralejo, Fuerteventura with the **Benchijigua** displaced from La Gomera and renamed the **Betancuria**. Another **Betancuria** took over in 1989, the **Buganvilla** followed in 1992 and the **Bocanya Express** has operated the route since 2003. The Austal Express 66 catamaran takes just 15 minutes to cross the Bocanya strait which separates the islands. *(Matt Davies)*

4 Ferrying in the Aegean
A first trip in Greek Waters by Richard Seville

The origins of the trip were way back in 1991; Christmas Eve to be exact. It was on that day, now 22 years ago, that I made my first and only sailings on the *Stena Horsa* between Folkestone and Boulogne. Having learnt that the route was to shut, as a 12 year old, I managed to convince my father to book a day trip to France so that I could experience one of the H-boats before their undoubted departure from the UK waters. It was my first international Sealink crossing and I was thoroughly taken with the ship. Despite a Force 8 gale raging, I enjoyed exploring the passenger facilities and even managed to secure a brief visit to the bridge. I was slightly disappointed to have missed the *Stena Hengist*, with both outward and return crossings on her sister, but the *Stena Horsa* immediately became a favourite. Knowing that the *Hengist* and *Horsa* were subsequently sold to Greece, throughout the 1990s, as I grew up I often wondered what had happened to them and eagerly awaited snippets of news in the shipping journals, not least in 'European Ferry Scene'.

Eight years later, a part-time job between studies provided enough income to anticipate a beach holiday and the thought arose of combining relaxing in the sun with the opportunity to catch up with the former Sealink twins. Leafing through holiday brochures finally allowed me to match the islands cited in shipping reports to a map, and to understand the geography of the Aegean islands. After much deliberation, I booked a fortnight on the island of Paros – a major Cycladic ferry hub – with a bargain basement and now long defunct tour operator. Ferry news, however, was always delayed and in the days before the Internet, the exact ships in service, and which routes and schedules they operated, were very difficult to establish from the UK. My primary aim was to sail on the former *Hengist*, having missed her on the Channel but although there was guaranteed to be a fascinating line-up, it was really a case of hoping that the-H-boats would be in service.

AEGEAN-BOUND

June 1999 therefore found me boarding a flight to the island of Mykonos, from where I would be escorted for a sea transfer to Paros itself. The first hurdle came when the planned transfer fell through due to capricious catamaran timetables and the tour guide announced that I would have to wait in Mykonos for eight hours before the transfer was possible. Frustration rapidly evaporated however as our coach arrived in Mykonos Town and the tiny harbour revealed the familiar profile of Agoudimos Lines' *Penelope A* – none other than the former *Stena Horsa*. She was lying over pending her afternoon return to the mainland port of Rafina, and alongside her was the modernised profile of Strintzis Lines' *Superferry II* – the former Belgian stalwart *Prince Laurent*. Soon, they were joined by the old Holyhead favourite *St Columba* as Agapitos Express Ferries' *Express Aphrodite* as well as the *Naias II* of Agapitos Lines – a ferry then entirely new to me, but which would become notorious a couple of years later as the sister to the ill-fated *Express Samina*. Walking around the breakwater, followed by the island's famed, if rather battered, pelican I was able to observe the trio at close quarters.

After spending the day exploring the whitewashed town and longingly gazing at the ferries coming and going, my transfer to the port of Parikia on Paros finally arrived. This was the Ceres hydrofoil *Mega Dolphin XXXII*, which I would later learn was built as the Spanish *Barracuda* for inter-island service in the Canaries. She called en route at Naxos, where we were overshadowed by the Louis Lines' cruise ship *Princesa Cypria*, originally DFDS' *Prinsesse Margrethe*, before finally arriving at Paros.

ARRIVAL AT PAROS

There, it was dark when I finally reached my studio apartment on the edge of town around the main bay. Ultimately, the best that could be said about it was that the location was convenient – 15 minutes' walk from the main waterfront and close to a small beach where the ferries could be observed in the distance coming and going. The apartment itself was basic to say the least; just a bed, ill-equipped kitchenette and nothing more than a hose for a shower. The grounds were still a building site, but at least the swimming pool was complete. For the price, it was probably unfair to complain too much. And that year, 1999, before the seismic changes to the domestic ferry industry brought about through the wave of consolidation in 2000, Paros was a ferry enthusiast's paradise. Dozens of different ferries would call in each day, in a myriad of colourful liveries, principally en route up or down the core island chain of the Central Cyclades. Paros is the first call on the route from the mainland, ahead of Naxos, Ios and then finally iconic Santorini. Rival companies competed intensely, with legendary Greek names such as Agapitos Lines, Agapitos Express Ferries, Arkadia Lines and Ceres. Most vessels were still North European veterans, as car-carrying high-speed craft and purpose-built fast conventional tonnage were still really yet to appear.

ON BOARD THE HENGIST

After a couple of days relaxing and exploring the town, I had validated that the former *Hengist* was indeed in service and was able to book a journey I had long anticipated – a crossing on her for the hour-long hop to adjoining Naxos. At the time, computer ticketing had recently been introduced but departures could only be ascertained by scouring the different chalkboards of the many agencies to be found around Parikia. The traditional agent's tricks reigned supreme – the next departure was always on their ship;

An array of veteran ferries lined up at Mykonos; including the **Superferry II**, previously the Belgian **Prince Laurent**, the arriving **Naias II**, and the former Folkestone stalwart **Horsa**, as Agoudimos Lines' **Penelope A**. This, and all the photographs, were taken in June 1999.

Captured swinging at Paros, the familiar profile of the **Express Apollon** is immediately recognisable as the former **Senlac**.

Photographed from the passing **Express Olympia** is her running mate, the **Express Santorini**, originally constructed as the French **Chartres**.

travellers wanting to understand the full picture needed to visit several different agencies in order to find schedules for all companies. Both first – or Distinguished-class and standard – or Economic-class tickets were sold on most sailings, the former with reserved access to a segregated lounge and occasionally restaurant. In the final years of the drachma, Economic fares were great value, tickets to Naxos costing just a few pounds and the longer voyage up to Piraeus being sold for approximately £10. The *Hengist* was then sailing for Agapitos Lines, under one of the most challenging ferry names ever recorded – the *Panagia Ekatontapiliani*, named after a famous church in Parikia, bestowed with 100 bells. With the day's first sailings heading out from Piraeus from 07.00, rush hour at Paros was around lunchtime, with a succession of competing ships calling in. Queuing up in the narrow marshalling sheds where passengers were corralled, I eagerly awaited the familiar profile of the *Hengist*. During a turnaround lasting no more than five minutes, a long line of passengers disembarked, and soon, the hordes were surging forward to board. I roved throughout her accommodation, which at that time was still essentially unchanged from her 1986/87 Sealink British Ferries' refit. I was delighted to be on board the ship I had missed so narrowly in 1991, especially as her interior accommodation was only lightly filled – most passengers preferring to be outside. I even managed a quick peek in her former Wessex Bar, now cordoned off as the Distinguished-class accommodation, and was delighted to find her famous Franta Belsky stairwell mural intact. All too soon, we were docking in Naxos, and just minutes later, the *Panagia Ekatontapiliani* had raised her ramp and was away.

The first task upon arrival was to secure tickets for my return later that day as tickets could still only be bought from the port of departure. The chalkboards revealed a tempting list of potential ships, and I settled on another Sealink veteran – this time the former *Earl Granville*, then sailing as Agapitos Express Ferries' *Express Olympia*. Before, however, I spent an enjoyable day exploring Naxos Town, wandering out to the Naxian arch overlooking the harbour and enjoying an evening meal overlooking the seafront. My late evening crossing formed part of the *Express Olympia*'s afternoon departure from Santorini, which would arrive back in Piraeus in the early morning. On board, she too retained many reminders from her Sealink career, being essentially unchanged from her later Channel Islands days with the Sealink insignia logo still to be found in various places.

THE 'ROI' TO SANTORINI

The next day trip from Paros was to be altogether more ambitious; a long excursion down to Santorini. Whilst lying on the beach close to my apartment, I had seen a completely unexpected profile calling in – none other than the former Belgian *Roi Baudouin* of 1965. Laid up in Piraeus since 1995, she had been the final remaining inactive vessel caught up in the collapse of Ventouris Sea Lines – news had not yet reached the UK of her return to service. In an all-white livery, she was operating a complex timetable of inter-island sailings from a base on Syros. Tracking down an agent representing her proved challenging with just a couple to be found selling tickets for the newly reactivated company. Each Tuesday, her schedule included a wondrous voyage from Paros to Santorini, not via the usual express route, but on a circuitous journey calling in at many small islands. This had to be done! With the poor sales network, and with eight hours on board for this crossing, it was not a service popular with the majority of tourists, and I virtually had her to myself. In addition to simply sunbathing on deck as we motored in and out of tiny, rocky, island harbours, I was free to explore her musty accommodation which retained much wooden panelling. I could even wander through her empty vehicle deck; where the aft ramp was left half open as we sailed along. Unusually, she was operating as a one-class ship and, with her cafeteria still mothballed, there was absolutely no catering on board except for the sale of ice cream.

After four hours ashore on the volcanic island, I retraced my steps to board the *Express Santorini* of Agapitos Express Ferries for our return journey. The former *Chartres* of SNCF, she presented quite a contrast to the other ships we had sampled for her passenger facilities had been comprehensively and most comfortably refurbished throughout with bright, colourful fabrics and new wooden laminate flooring. Nonetheless, a couple of

Unloading at Paros, the **Express Hermes** was soon to reload and head back up to Piraeus.

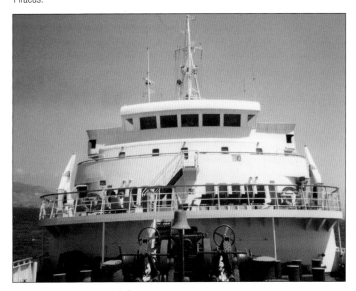

Taken from the prow of the **Express Hermes**; her original identity as the **Princesse Astrid** was still to be found on her bell.

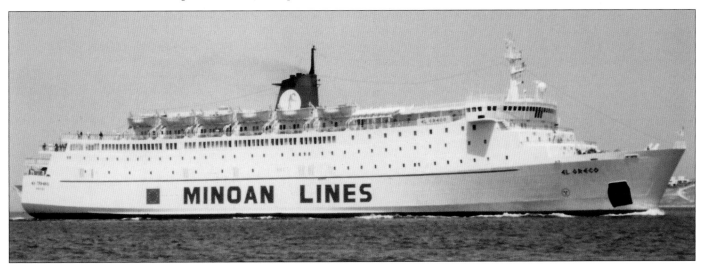

One of the many ferries calling in at Paros was Minoan Lines' **El Greco**; serving a lengthy route from Thessaloniki down to Santorini.

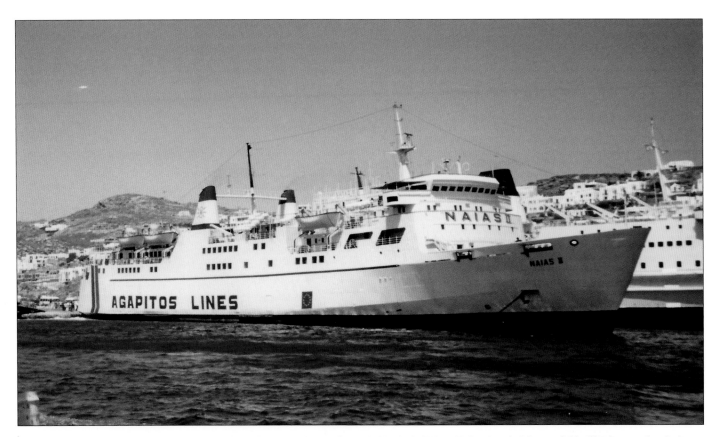

Agapitos Lines' ran a diverse fleet in 1999, including the **Naias II**, constructed as the **Comte de Nice** for SNCM in 1966, her sister the infamous **Golden Vergina**, as well as the former Sealink units **Hengist** and **Earl Harald**.

A busy scene at Piraeus, as the **Naias Express** (formerly the **Ailsa Princess** & **Earl Harold**) approaches her berth adjacent to the **Express Apollon**. The **Romilda**, previously the **Pride of Canterbury** of 1974, is in the background.

surprising reminders from her original career did remain – a huge painting of Dieppe harbour still hung overlooking her forward stairwell, and another quick visit to the Distinguished-class lounge revealed a wooden bas relief of Chartres Cathedral. At the opposite end of the scale, trays bearing the Sealink Stena Line logo were still in use in one of the bars.

In between the occasional ferry trips, I continued a normal island holiday, exploring Paros by hire car and visiting places such as the Butterfly Valley at Petaloudes and the hillside town of Lefkes. I also caught a local tourist caique to the nearby island of Anti-Paros, where I enjoyed visiting the famous chambered cave with impressive stalagmites and stalactites – descending into the dank gloom providing a welcome respite from the heat – before simply paddling along the waters of the deserted local beach. Close by, a small fleet of landing craft car ferries came and went, providing a vehicle service to Punta on Paros.

Piraeus

Although most of my two weeks was unplanned, one element which I had prearranged was a two-night visit to Athens. I had booked hotel accommodation in advance, and just needed to arrange the ferry crossings to and from Paros. My outward sailing was once again on board the *Express Olympia*, a superb, lightly loaded early afternoon departure. Having left Paros, I ate lunch in the restaurant – still bearing the name the Carteret Restaurant and still containing the long defunct buffet serveries from the days of the all-inclusive Starliner service to the Channel Islands as well as the vignettes of different English Earls on the bulkheads. Early evening saw the ship approach Piraeus, and I waited on deck with great anticipation at sailing into this legendary ferry port. I was not to be disappointed; the quaysides thronged with fascinating tonnage. As we approached the Great Harbour, we were passed by the *Romilda* of GA Ferries – the former *Pride of Canterbury* of 1974 which I had seen back in 1991 at Boulogne, from the *Stena Horsa*. I stood on deck, camera constantly clicking, as we manoeuvred to our berth passing all manner of ferries, intriguingly including the *Hermes* of Access Ferries, formerly the *Nils Holgersson* of 1967, as well as her successor, the *Nils Holgersson* of 1974 as NEL Line's *Theofilos*.

Disembarking into the chaos that constantly reigns in Piraeus was exhilarating if slightly daunting; crowds rushing here and there, a myriad of purposeful journeys, constant bustling traffic, honking horns, all overseen by traffic policeman and smartly uniformed port officials surveying their fiefdom, with ships' whistles occasionally piercing the cacophony. Once again, the first task was to book a return passage a few days later and I wandered around the multitude of ticket agencies close to the quayside, browsing the handwritten chalkboards, admiring the dusty models to be found, and establishing the different options. Despite debating an elongated return via Mykonos in order to sail on the former *St Columba*, I eventually settled on a late afternoon departure of the *Express Apollon,* and then headed to the subway in the far corner of the Great Harbour to make my way to Athens itself.

The *Express Apollon* was built as the *Senlac*, the third of Sealink's H-boats, delivered in 1973 for the Newhaven to Dieppe service. I arrived early in Piraeus two days later, to board promptly and soon I was striding her decks, exploring her accommodation one minute, whilst rushing outside to photograph the bustling maritime scene the next. On the berth adjacent was her sister, the *Panagia Ekatontapiliani*, loading for a rival departure down the Central Cycladic chain. Just around the corner was the *Milos Express*, their design cousin and one-time fleetmate, the former *Vortigern*, which I almost missed as she heaved up her anchors and sailed past en route to the Western Cyclades. If that were not enough of a sight for a Sealink enthusiast's eyes, shortly afterwards the one-time *Ailsa Princess* and later *Earl Harold* motored into the Great Harbour shortly afterwards and tied up right alongside us. The *Express Apollon* herself was somewhat of a British Rail time warp; although she had been comfortably refitted in parts, there were many reminders of her original identity including signs in the classic BR-typeface, directing travellers to the Tea Bar for example. Fibreglass bas relief panels in her cafeteria depicted scenes from the Battle of Hastings, whilst in her forward stairwell the full Franta Belsky mural remained, including the signature Senlac panel.

FINAL DAY TRIP

My fortnight's holiday was rapidly drawing to a close, but I managed to make one final day trip back to Naxos. The key objective in doing so was to catch the later sister of the *Roi Baudouin*, the *Princesse Astrid* of 1968, which after sailing with Ventouris Sea Lines alongside her sister for many years, had been rescued after their collapse and returned to service in the Agapitos Express Ferries fleet as *Express Hermes*. My outward passage, however, was on a vessel I had never previously heard of – the diminutive *Syros Express*. Dating from 1970, she was a classic example of a locally built early car ferry, with a quirky appearance and decidedly slow service speed. Commissioned by Nomikos Lines as their *Aegeus*, she was currently being used for local inter-island services and fulfilled all of the stereotypes of the Greek ferry, running constantly behind schedule. Whereas most ferries managed the short hop to Naxos in about an hour, the *Syros Express* was scheduled for two! However, she provided a convenient mid-morning departure ahead of the regular ships heading down from the mainland. On board, she offered two small saloons one atop of the other, forward of her small garage, above which there was a broad sundeck lined with wooden benches. She succeeded in capturing a fair slice of traffic on offer, and almost everyone headed straight for the sundeck leaving her air-conditioned saloons empty. Despite her slow progress, she offered an enjoyable sail, closely hugging the Northern coast of Paros.

One lunch and a few hours' exploring later, and I was waiting for the *Express Hermes*. Whilst her earlier sister had exclusively served the Aegean since her sale to Greece, the former *Princesse Astrid* had originally been deployed on the Adriatic, only transferring later to sail out of Rafina for a different faction of the warring Ventouris dynasty. Later sold to Agapitos Express Ferries, she had been comfortably modernised internally and presented a substantially different impression than the little changed *Georgios*

Alongside in Piraeus were Japanese conversions **Lato** of ANEK and **King Minos** of the Minoan Lines, both awaiting overnight departures to Crete.

One of the many unexpected vessels to be seen in Greece was the former SNCM freighter **Monte D'Oro** of 1972; shown alongside at Naxos as the **Macedonia II**.

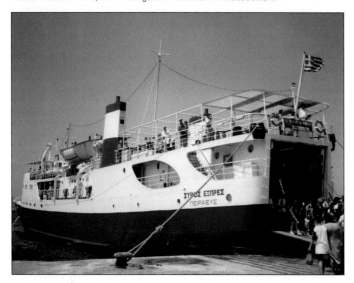

The ungainly **Syros Express** rattled around the islands, typically very late.

Express. Her forward lounge had become the Distinguished-class facility, retaining the wooden panelling, but attractively refitted with fittings finished in burgundy and pale yellow. Amidships, the traditional side lounges remained, but aft the former restaurant had been converted into a modern cafe, whilst an additional lounge bar had been built on the deck above. Despite the extensive conversion, happily, her original bell could still be found on her foredeck.

The former Belgian was lightly loaded, and made an excellent last hurrah for my first experience of Greece. It was not the final crossing of the trip – that was reserved for the modern catamaran *SeaJet 2* of Strintzis Lines which carried me back to Mykonos for the flight home – but the *Express Hermes* rounded off a superb fortnight catching up with the veteran ferries in operation in the area. Despite the somewhat dubious accommodation, it had been a great holiday. It had been a fascinating experience, not just from a ferry point of view, as I was equally charmed with the Cyclades and the Greek island way of life. From the ferry perspective, I sampled the Greek domestic market just before a period of significant change – huge consolidation amongst operators lay ahead the following year with the creation of Hellas Ferries, as well as other developments such as fully computerised ticketing. With a tally of nine individual ships – of which six had previously seen service on the English Channel – I certainly was delighted with what I had achieved. It was to prove the foundation for more extensive travels in the years ahead. Today, 15 years later, only four of the ships survive with six having been scrapped. The *Mega Dolphin XXXII* is believed to be long laid up in the environs of Perama, and the *Sea Jet 2* continues for Sea Jets. Most happily, however, the *Hengist* remains a stalwart of the Cyclades as the *Agios Georgios* – although after an all too brief return to service at Rafina in 2013, the *Penelope A* was sadly withdrawn.

5 Saga Sapphire
Photo feature by John Mavin

When, in late 2009, the *Saga Rose* finally retired from service, there was much speculation as to what would replace her as flagship of Saga Cruises' fleet. The company had acquired the former *Astoria* which entered service as the *Saga Pearl 2* following an impressive refurbishment. However, a larger ship was clearly required and towards the end of 2010 the rumour mill indicated that the company was negotiating the purchase of the *Bleu de France*. This was finally confirmed and the ship would be re-named *Saga Sapphire*.

EUROPA

Originally built by Bremer Vulkan in 1981 for Hapag-Lloyd as the *Europa*, she was at that time one of the largest passenger ships afloat. With the accommodation over seven decks and situated in the forward sections, she offered a high standard of luxury cruising for the mainly German market.

Between her building and her acquisition by Saga, she had undergone various changes of name and two major refits. Her history is well documented elsewhere but suffice to say she has an impressive record.

I suppose the first reaction to the news of the purchase would be the question...is she too big for Saga? At over 37,000 gross tons she was considerably larger than 'Rose' and 'Ruby', and with a passenger capacity of 706, some questioned if that special Saga touch might be compromised. I think that this fear has been quickly dispelled, largely due to the efforts of Saga's excellent design team who have the remarkable gift of really knowing their customers.

Prior to entering service with Saga the ship was re-fitted at the Fincantieri shipyard at Palermo, but unfortunately industrial action at the yard delayed her inaugural cruise. Another major setback occurred after the cruise finally got underway – at Valencia a fault was discovered in the port engine cooling system and, as repairs would take quite a few days, the cruise had to be abandoned – not a welcome turn of events for anyone.

Further problems were encountered during the first season, the most noticeable being with the generators. Other criticisms were directed at the air-conditioning system and unpleasant odours in various parts of the accommodation.

There is no way one can obfuscate the disappointment and frustration felt with these initial problems but recent reviews indicate a high level of customer satisfaction with the 'Sapphire' – "bedding in nicely" as one seasoned cruiser told me.

ON BOARD

When the *Saga Sapphire* made her first arrival at Dover in May 2012 your Editor and I went aboard to see for ourselves. As our visit fitted in between passenger debark and embark the ship

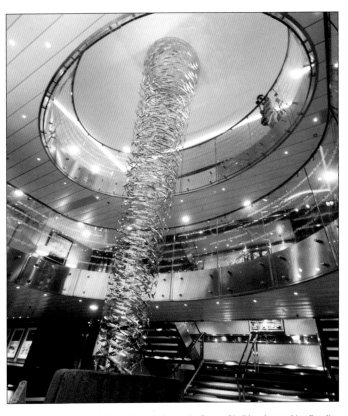

Large holes had to be cut through two decks, and a fireproof bulkhead moved to allow it to be installed, but this is Shoal by Scabetti.

was very busy, particularly in the accommodation areas. Nonetheless, we had ample time for a good look around the more public areas.

The hull and superstructure colour remains the same but gone is the trademark yellow Saga funnel which is now a pale blue with a different logo on each side. Boarding the ship on Deck 5 you walk into the newly constructed Atrium which features Shoal, a stunning seven-metre display by Scabetti that rises over three decks.

I don't think I'm alone when I say that an important Saga feature is open deck space. This to me is a fundamental requirement of a sea cruise, and on the 'Sapphire' there is plenty of it to suit the most enthusiastic promenader!

Particularly noticeable are the different themes of the lounges, bars and restaurants. Although the whole ship has been given a distinctly traditional English feel, such as the Aviator's and Cooper's Bars, the pan-cultural themes of the main restaurants allow one's imagination to go where it pleases. I loved the absence of huge spaces and the feeling of always wondering what was going to be around the next corner.

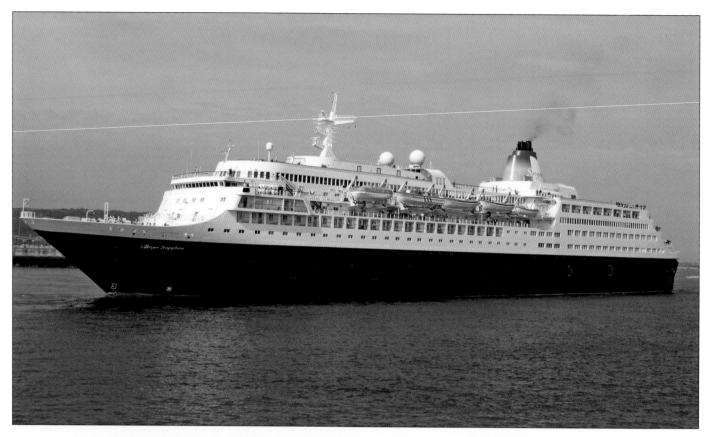

The new look for Saga - the **Saga Sapphire** at Dover in June 2013.

The inaugural arrival of the **Saga Sapphire** at Dover on 21st May 2012. Bad weather seemed to be a feature of her early arrivals at the Kentish port.

In June 2013 she arrived to join her (sadly) soon to be retired fleetmate **Saga Ruby** – in characteristically awful weather!

Looking aft on Deck 12. The deck below features the outdoor swimming pool and games area. Moving forward are a spacious observation area over the Drawing Room.

There is always something to read on a Saga ship. This is part of the very well-stocked library which then leads into the Drawing Room.

An impressive Banyan Tree root display at the entrance to the Drawing Room where, as well as having a bar and larder (snack bar), there are large observation windows looking out over the ship's bow. The Drawing Room is also where computers and I-Pads are provided – and very popular they are with Saganauts!

Above & below: Styled to the theme of different continents, the main Pole to Pole Restaurant will seat 620 passengers. To avoid one big and noisy room of the type found on many ships it is cleverly divided into eight more intimate areas, each with décor reflecting the region represented. Some early customer comments questioned the logistics of the service arrangements but it seems that these problems have now been addressed.

The Grill – this informal dining venue is the place to take a lighter meal and watch your food being cooked in the state of the art show kitchen. The Grill leads out to the Verandah on Deck 9 where, weather permitting, guests can eat outside.

The smaller East to West is a 64-seat restaurant that specialises in Indian, Sri Lankan and Thai cuisine of an exceptionally high standard. Meals here have to be booked in advance and the décor, with its traditional carvings, is really very impressive.

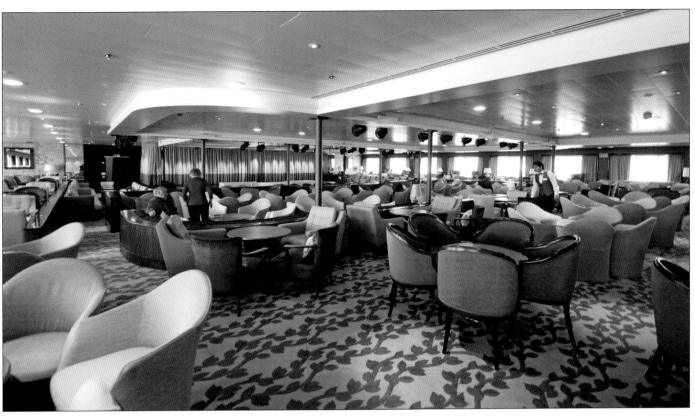

The Britannia Lounge is the ship's main entertainment venue which offers a variety of musicial events and cabarets in the evenings. It is also a multi-purpose daytime space for afternoon tea, lectures, dancing lessons, chin-wags and any other indoor group activities.

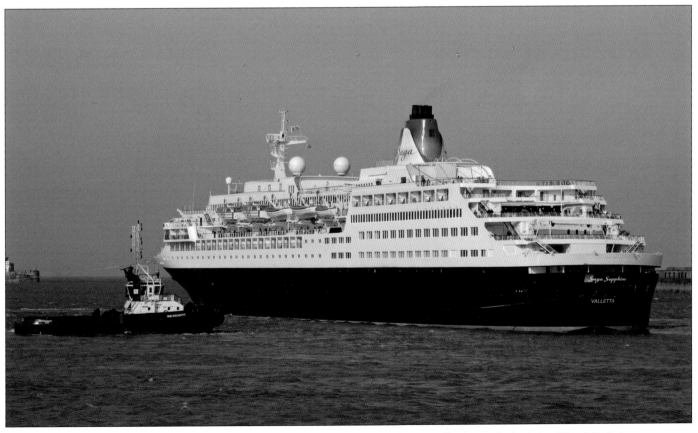

Because of the wind, the **Saga Sapphire** breaks with the normal practice of leaving via Dover's Western Entrance and heads across the bay to depart through the East.

6 Kingswear Castle

by Richard Clammer

Recognised as a 'vessel of pre-eminent national significance' within the National Historic Fleet, the delightful little River Dart paddle steamer *Kingswear Castle* is one of Britain's most successful but understated operational preservation stories. Having been purchased and restored by the Paddle Steamer Preservation Society and spent 28 seasons quietly but efficiently providing public excursions on the Medway and Thames, she returned to the river of her birth during December 2012 and has just completed her first season back in Devon waters, operating the very services for which she was designed. It is, perhaps, a good moment to review her remarkable history.

Launched in 1924 by Philip & Son Ltd from their Noss Shipyard on the banks of the Dart, the *Kingswear Castle* was the very last of a long line of distinctive paddle steamers built to maintain a river service between Dartmouth and Totnes. Until the arrival of the railways in the mid-1800s, both of these relatively isolated towns suffered from the widespread contemporary problem of poor land communications and the 11-mile navigable portion of the River Dart provided the most convenient route for trade passing between the two or onward into the hinterland. Passengers were catered for by sailing 'passage boats' until, in 1836, the first steamship appeared on the river.

This tiny vessel, the itinerant 31-ton *Paul Pry*, which had previously operated on the River Wye, the Mersey and the Menai Straits, arrived just as the channel up to Totnes had been dredged and improved but was reported to be in a "shattered state" and lasted for only one season. In 1837, she was replaced by the short-lived *Dart* and later by the *Undine* and *Violante*. Things remained relatively settled on the river until 1854 when a local

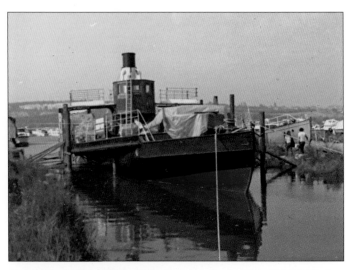

On the slipway at Medway Bridge Marina during her epic restoration which lasted from 1972 until 1982. *(PSPS Archive)*

gentleman named Charles Seale Hayne inherited his father's considerable fortune and set about developing various business interests in the area. Foremost among these was the promotion of the Dartmouth & Torbay Railway Company which was intended to extend the South Devon Railway's Torquay branch to a new terminus at Kingswear with a ferry link across to Dartmouth. In anticipation of obtaining the lucrative ferry rights and benefiting from increased river trade, Hayne and his partner John Moody introduced the new *Louisa* on to the river in 1856 in direct competition with the *Dartmouth* owned by a consortium headed by his arch political and commercial rival, Arthur Howe Holdsworth, Governor of Dartmouth Castle and local MP. Both companies added additional ships to their fleet and engaged in spirited rivalry until, as the railway crept ever closer to Kingswear, Holdsworth's camp withdrew from the fray. Hayne and Moody sold their shares in their ships to the newly incorporated Dartmouth Steam Packet Co. Ltd which, unsurprisingly, was granted a long lease to operate the ferry to Dartmouth and sole use of the pontoons on both sides of the river. By the time the railway opened in August 1864, the brand new river steamer *Newcomin* and the ferry boat *Perseverance* had been added to the fleet and Hayne's companies virtually controlled the river trade as well as introducing a short-lived and unsuccessful cross-Channel service from Kingswear to the Channel Islands and St Malo using the steamer *Eclair*.

FLEET EXPANSION

In 1876 the Great Western Railway took over the operation of the line to Kingswear and the ferry to Dartmouth, and Seal Hayne's Dartmouth Steam Packet Company sold its steamers to

A brand new and well-laden **Kingswear Castle** makes a fine sight as she steams downstream towards Dartmouth Castle, as built she was not fitted with the raised landing platforms on either side of her wheelhouse. *(Author's collection)*

Off on another cruise, the **Kingswear Castle** has just departed from her Medway base at Thunderbolt Pier within the Chatham Historic Dockyard and is just about to pass the privately owned steam coaster **VIC56** on 27th May 2012. *(Richard Clammer)*

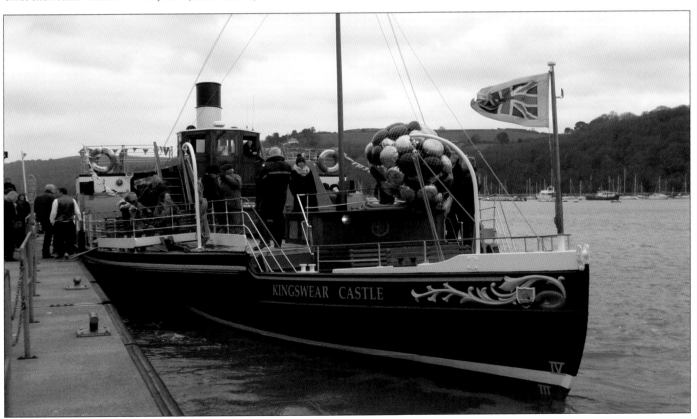

The **Kingswear Castle** embarking passengers at Dartmouth pontoon prior to her inaugural sailing on the Dart, Good Friday 29th March 2013. Despite almost arctic temperatures and a strong north easterly wind, the sailing was a huge success and the balloons, in the ship's funnel colours, were released near the harbour mouth. *(Richard Clammer)*

a syndicate of local businessmen who formed the Dartmouth & Torbay Steam Packet Co. Ltd. The new group retained the river steamers *Dartmouth* and *Newcomin*, sold the paddle tugs *Guide* and *Pilot* and added the small screw steamers *Hauley* and *Nimble*. Then, in 1880, they took delivery of their first major river steamer, the *Berry Castle*, from Messrs Polyblank's yard in Waterhead Creek at Kingswear.

The *Berry Castle* is highly significant as the ship upon which both the design and the 'Castle' nomenclature of all subsequent Dart paddle steamers, including the *Kingswear Castle*, was based. Her boiler and funnel were positioned slightly abaft the paddle boxes, between which the wheel was situated. From her open upper deck curving stairways led down onto the low well decks fore and aft, from which access to the saloons was gained by way of varnished companionways. This distinctive design was found only on the Dart and the neighbouring Kingsbridge Estuary and was refined in each subsequent ship built for the company. The *Dartmouth Castle* of 1885, *Kingswear Castle* of 1904 and *Dartmouth Castle (II)* of 1907 all followed the same pattern, although the smaller *Totnes Castle* of 1896, which was intended for the winter service, was built with a continuous upper deck

and no wells.

In 1906 the D. & T.S.P.Co. was re-incorporated as the River Dart Steamboat Co. and the steamers' black funnel colouring replaced by a more cheerful yellow with a black top. In 1914, the *Totnes Castle* was sold for further service in Dorset and replaced by the *Compton Castle* which took the local design to its next stage. Unlike her predecessors, her upper deck was extended outwards over elongated paddle sponsons, greatly increasing her deck space; she had portholes in place of the usual saloon windows and was fitted with a raised passenger deck above her aft well deck.

Passenger services continued throughout the First World War, albeit at a reduced level, and the return of peace saw the traditional combination of summer excursions and year-round service between Dartmouth and Totnes which paused off Dittisham and Bow Creek to collect and set down passengers and goods from open boats. As road transport improved, however, the popularity of the year-round service waned and by the late 1920s it had been withdrawn altogether allowing the steamers to concentrate completely on the growing seasonal excursion trade. The delightful village of Dittisham was a very popular destination

The **Kingswear Castle** being repainted on the Dartmouth Steam Railway & River Boat Company's covered slipway in Old Mill Creek on 1st March 2013. This is the very shipyard where she was maintained throughout her first career on the river. *(Richard Clammer)*

The **Kingswear Castle** passing the hulk of her namesake predecessor of 1904, which is beached at Fleet Mill Cove, just below Totnes. *(Richard Clammer)*

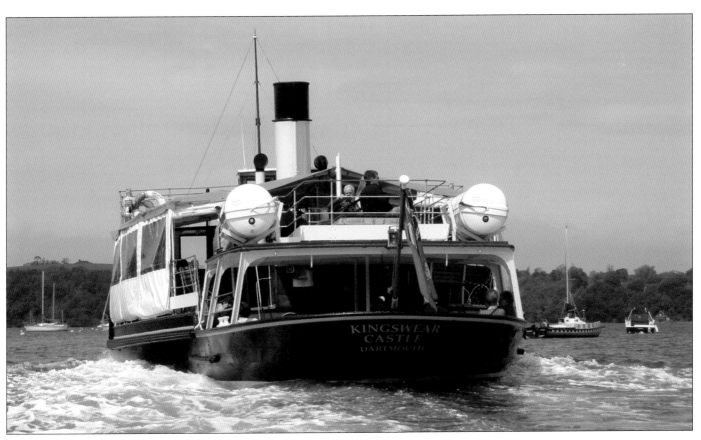

A stern view of the **Kingswear Castle** as she approaches the Flat Owers buoy, her upstream turning point on harbour cruises. *(Richard Clammer)*

The **Kingswear Castle** steams downstream amid the sylvan scenery of the upper river, 19th June 2013. *(Richard Clammer)*

The **Kingswear Castle** steams through Dartmouth Harbour on one of her regular harbour cruises, 20th May 2013. *(Richard Clammer)*

and in 1922 the company completed a long pier which stretched out to the low-water mark and allowed the Totnes-bound steamers to call at all states of the tide. The company's second motor vessel, the diminutive *Dittisham Castle* was built specifically to maintain a shuttle service between Dartmouth and the new pier.

In 1923 additional shares were issued in order to finance the construction of two new paddlers, the *Totnes Castle* and *Kingswear Castle* which entered service in 1923 and 1924 respectively. The two ships were built from the same plans by Messrs Philip & Son, and were almost identical to the 1914 *Compton Castle* from Cox & Co. of Falmouth. They measured 108ft between perpendiculars (113 overall) x 17.6ft (28ft over the paddle boxes) and drew 3ft of water. Constructed of steel, they were 91 and 94 gross tons respectively and were fitted with two-cylinder compound diagonal engines. The *Totnes Castle*'s were constructed by Philip, but the *Kingswear Castle* was fitted with the machinery from her namesake predecessor, the *Kingswear Castle (I)* of 1904.

The older ship had re-entered service after the 1914-18 War but in 1923 had been sold to the Port Sanitary Authority for use as a floating isolation hospital in Dartmouth Harbour. Stripped of her machinery and with a number of ugly deckhouses constructed on her upper deck, she served in that capacity until 1927, when unsuccessful attempts were made to sell her as a houseboat. Eventually she was towed upriver and beached at Fleet Mill, just below Totnes, where her hull can still be seen to this day.

KINGSWEAR CASTLE

The new *Kingswear Castle* therefore entered an excursion fleet consisting of her near sisters *Totnes Castle* and *Compton Castle*, the paddler *Dartmouth Castle* of 1907 and the smaller motor ships *Berry Castle* and *Dittisham Castle*. The *Dartmouth Castle* had her upper deck carried out over new, extended sponsons and was fitted with a wheelhouse and raised aft deck to bring her appearance into line with the newer paddlers. As things turned out, the *Kingswear Castle* was the last paddle steamer ever built for the River Dart and thus represented the ultimate development of an intensely local design which was to become as familiar a part of the Dart scenery as the landscape itself.

During the 1920s and 30s the leisurely cruise 'Up and Down the River Dart' became a major tourist attraction, with circular tours available in conjunction with the Great Western Railway and various local char-a-banc operators plus connecting sailings from Torquay and Exmouth provided by the Devon Dock, Pier & Steamship Co.'s paddle steamers *Duke of Devonshire* and *Duchess of Devonshire*. The lower reaches of the river were often packed with laid-up shipping and Dartmouth harbour itself was always alive with ferries, naval vessels and visiting merchant ships, in stark contrast to the sylvan upper reaches where oak woods tumbled down to the riverside.

In 1927 a 70ft steel motor vessel called *Clifton Castle* was added to the fleet, followed in 1937 and 1938 by the wooden *Greenway Castle* and *Seymour Castle*. The outbreak of war in September 1939 saw all pleasure sailings suspended. The

The aft saloon looking towards the steps which lead through a low deckhouse containing further toilets up onto the aft well deck. Although its bar is not currently used on a regular basis, the saloon whose white panelling is picked out in gold, is a tranquil space and ideal for private functions. *(Richard Clammer)*

A good crowd of passengers enjoy the early summer sunshine as the **Kingswear Castle** paddles upstream, 20th May 2013. *(Richard Clammer)*

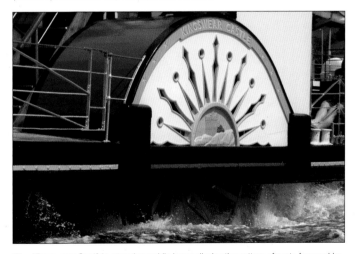

The **Kingswear Castle**'s attractive paddle boxes display the pattern of vents favoured by most of the Dart paddle steamers as well as a magnificent carved portrait of the eponymous castle. Each of her scarlet paddle wheels has twelve fixed, wooden floats which beat out a distinctive rhythm. *(Richard Clammer)*

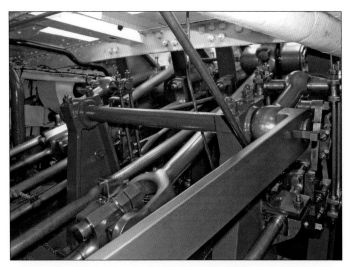

The compound diagonal main engine built in 1904 by Cox & Co of Falmouth for the first **Kingswear Castle** and transferred to the current ship in 1924. *(Richard Clammer)*

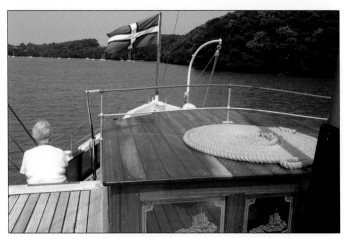

The view forward from **Kingswear Castle**'s upper deck. The low forward deckhouse, with its immaculate varnish work, was built during the winter of 2011-12 to replace its ageing predecessor. Entry to the forward saloon was originally via the curving steps on either side of the ship and through a doorway in the forward end of the deckhouse, which also houses two of the ship's splendid toilets. Note the shining brass and the Devon flag flying from the jack staff. *(Richard Clammer)*

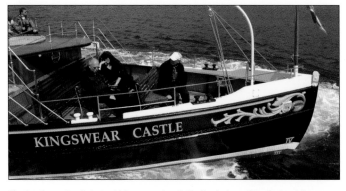

The low forward well-deck which was such a distinctive feature of the Dart paddlers, can be seen clearly in this view. The doorway leading into the forward saloon was originally located beneath the overhanging deck of the deckhouse, but was closed off in 2005 and replaced by a more convenient but less beautiful entry from the upper deck. This was done partly for the convenience of less mobile passengers but largely to remove any possibility of the more boisterous seas of the Thames and Medway splashing over the bulwarks and entering the saloon. *(Richard Clammer)*

Kingswear Castle was initially laid up but during 1940 was moored on the buoys off Kingswear and deputised briefly for the GWR Dartmouth to Kingswear ferry steamer *The Mew* which had set off towards Dunkirk. Along with the *Totnes Castle* she was also hired annually until 1954 to maintain the ferry crossing while *The Mew* was undergoing her annual refit. In the summer of 1941 permission was obtained to run a limited number of pleasure trips, and the two paddlers, as the only ships still in peacetime colours, brought a little joy and normality to the hearts of local residents as they thrashed their way up and down the river. A further period of lay-up followed until 1944 when allied invasion forces were gathering all along the south coast in the run-up to D-Day and the *Kingswear Castle* was re-activated to act as a tender for the U.S. Navy.

The return of peace saw a somewhat diminished fleet. The *Greenway* and *Clifton Castles* had both been sold and the paddler *Dartmouth Castle*, which had laid inactive throughout the war, was stripped of her fittings and buried in the bank at the company's Old Mill Creek shipyard where she acts as a landing stage to this day. Her wheelhouse, lifeboat and rails were fitted to a new motor ship of the same name which was launched in 1948 by Philip & Son who, a year later, also provided a new *Berry Castle* to replace her namesake which was sold to the Dutch in 1947.

The three paddlers and three motor vessels settled back into their old, familiar seasonal routine. Behind the scenes, however, significant changes were taking place and in 1952 Evans & Reid Investment Co. Ltd of Cardiff acquired a controlling interest in the River Dart Steamboat Company. Despite the loss in 1954 of the lucrative contract to provide one of the paddlers to relieve *The Mew* on the Dartmouth-Kingswear ferry, the new owners embarked upon a programme of fleet modernisation which was to spell the end for the three paddlers.

TWILIGHT OF THE PADDLERS

At the end of 1962 it was announced that the *Compton Castle* would require extensive repairs in order to have her certificates renewed and the company opted instead to have a new, steel motor vessel built by Philips. Completed in time for the 1963 season, she was named *Conway Castle* and inherited the rails from *Compton Castle* which was sold for further use as a cafe at Kingsbridge. The old paddler was subsequently moved to Looe and then to Lemon Quay at Truro where her hull was used for various retail ventures and remains to this day. Her engine is on show at the Blackgang Chine visitor attraction on the Isle of Wight.

During 1963 it was revealed that *Totnes Castle* required £6,000 of repairs to pass her survey and the decision was made to replace her with a sister ship to *Conway Castle*. Built by Bolsons of Poole she entered service in 1964 sporting the old paddler's wheelhouse and rails. The *Totnes Castle* was converted into an accommodation ship for a sailing school and moored in Dartmouth harbour but the venture failed and she was sold for breaking up at Plymouth in November 1967. However, she escaped this ignominious end by foundering en route in Bigbury Bay where she still provides a popular destination for divers.

Arriving at Dartmouth pontoon, 20th May 2013, with the **Dart Venturer** moored astern. *(Richard Clammer)*

Thus, at the beginning of the 1964 season, the *Kingswear Castle* was the only paddle steamer remaining in the company's fleet. Her boiler had been renewed and her hull partially re-plated during 1962 so she was in far better condition than her late sisters but as a coal-fired ship within a diesel fleet she was an inconvenient anachronism and it was clear that her days were numbered. The wet and windy summer of 1965 reduced her passenger loadings and sealed her fate. She was withdrawn early, towards the end of August, and the directors' report announced that "she has become quite uneconomic to maintain or operate and will be disposed of at the first advantageous opportunity."

The *Kingswear Castle* retreated to her lay-up berth in Old Mill Creek and it seemed to most observers that the beat of paddle wheels would never be heard on the Dart again. The fledgling Paddle Steamer Preservation Society (PSPS), however, had different ideas and realised that the ship's small size and recent repairs made her the most practical British candidate for preservation. The society expressed its interest to the River Dart Steamboat Co. but, with few members and very limited resources, was unable to proceed with the purchase until more

funds could be raised or a charterer found who would take initial responsibility for the ship.

Remarkably, Alan and Colin Ridett who had already purchased the redundant paddle steamer *Medway Queen* as the club house and centrepiece of their embryonic marina on the River Medina, agreed to charter the ship and arrange to have her towed to the Isle of Wight. The River Dart Steamboat Co. generously agreed to sell the ship for a mere £600 due to "sentiment and the fact that the old vessel is the last of the line" and on 20th June 1967 she was formally purchased by Paddle Steam Navigation Ltd, a company set up by the PSPS for that purpose.

Following slipping at Old Mill Creek for painting and closing up, the *Kingswear Castle* left the Dart under tow, presumably for the last time, and arrived at Cowes on 28th August. Although the Ridetts kept her machinery in good order and steamed her in the Solent on two occasions during 1969, her inaccessible mid-river berth made it difficult for PSPS volunteers to undertake any significant maintenance. Experiencing difficulties with their marina development and having failed to announce any cogent

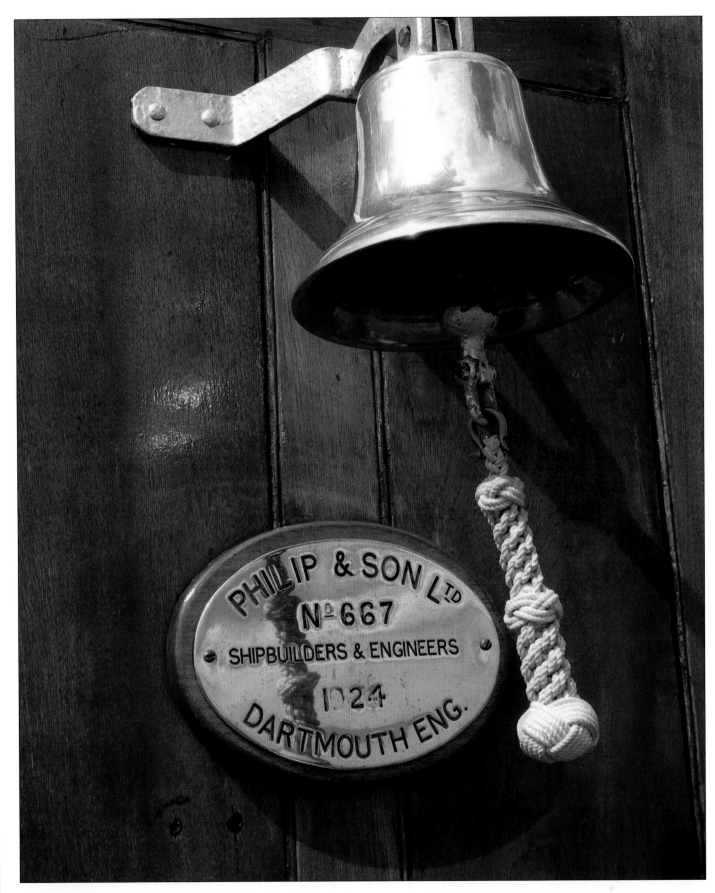

The builders' plate and ship's bell. *(Richard Clammer)*

plans for the ship's future use, the Ridetts moved her to a mud berth on the riverbank where she quickly began to suffer from vandalism.

Aware that she was deteriorating rapidly, the PSPS terminated the charter agreement and moved the ship down to Cowes where she spent the winter of 1970. On 16th June 1971 she left Cowes towed by the tug *Dagger* for the voyage to the River Medway where one of the PSPS's officers had offered her a berth in his Medway Bridge Marina. She arrived safely two days later but was still not out of trouble as the tow had used up most of the Society's slender resources and nothing remained for her restoration. By December 1972 the Society's committee was forced to recommend her sale to the highest bidder but, as so often happens, the crisis engendered a new sense of determination to see her survive.

A small but hard-working band of volunteers led by project leader Laurie Beale stepped forward and began the immense task of restoration. With hindsight one can only gasp at the size of the task they took on and conquered. Over the next eight years much wasted steelwork was reinforced or replaced, decks re-laid and re-caulked, paddlewheels removed, shafts drawn, paddle boxes and wheelhouse rebuilt and much, much more. By 1979, the PSPS was in a position to fund some professional assistance while several local firms provided materials and labour free of charge and the task forged ahead. In November 1982, the boiler was steamed and the engine turned over for the first time in 13 years and on the weekend of 4th-6th November 1983 the ship successfully completed steaming trials on the Medway. The impossible had been achieved!

PRESERVATION

Having restored the ship to operational condition, a decision had to be made as to what to do with her next to secure her future. In the short term it was decided to operate her on a limited commercial basis carrying a maximum of 12 passengers per trip on sailings along the Medway during the summer of 1984. Crewed entirely by volunteers, she operated public sailings and charters on an average of two days per week from Strood Pier, steamed round to the Thames where she became the star attraction at Gravesend Edwardian Fair and rendezvoused for the first time with the PSPS's other paddle steamer the *Waverley*. The *Kingswear Castle* had proved mechanically reliable, much practical experience had been gained, and the directors concluded that, if she was to become financially viable, the only way forward was to seek a full passenger certificate in order to re-enter full public service in 1985.

During the winter of 1984/85 the ship underwent further work to upgrade the saloons and make her fully compliant with D.T.I. regulations. John Megoran was appointed as full-time Master and manager, an agreement was reached with the Historic dockyard at Chatham to operate from Thunderbolt Pier and, on 16th May, the ship was issued with class V and VI D.T.I. passenger certificates for 250 and 100 passengers respectively. She made her first full trip on 18th May on charter to the Coastal Cruising Association and entered public service the following day. Her programme consisted of cruises on the

Medway from Chatham and Strood, regular trips from Southend (although she was not initially permitted to carry passengers across the estuary from the Medway to Southend) together with visits to London, Whitstable and special trips to view the Tall Ships Race and barge matches.

During the following winter an invitation was received to return the ship to the Dart to run in conjunction with the Dart Valley Railway. The idea of returning the ship to her correct historical setting where she could operate as part of an established fleet held great appeal and the plan was given close consideration. In the end various practical considerations made it impossible to proceed during 1986 but the idea surfaced repeatedly in the years ahead and eventually came to fruition in December 2012.

Meanwhile, the *Kingswear Castle* settled into what was to become an amazingly successful 28-year career on the River Medway. As well as being an excellent ship-handler, John Megoran proved to be an adroit and energetic manager and a fine ambassador for the ship. He spent his winter months promoting the ship at travel fairs, obtaining private charters and advanced bookings from coach operators and ensuring that she was widely advertised throughout the South East. Business grew steadily and her core offering of short cruises from Chatham and Strood was enlivened by a programme of fascinating full-day trips through the Swale to Whitstable, round the Isle of Sheppey, upriver to Snodland, across to Southend and elsewhere. Between 1984 and 2005 she went at least once a year to London, carrying passengers to and from the Medway on her positioning trips and offering cruises from various of the capital's piers in between. In 2000 she made a unique call at the Millennium Pier beside the London Eye and in 2002 became the first paddle steamer to visit Putney Pier for 70 years. The unexpected closure of Strood Pier during 2005 was cushioned to some extent by an increase in sailings from Rochester on the other side of the Medway. Pre-booked afternoon tea cruises, evening jazz cruises, wedding receptions, barge races, 'Learn to operate a paddle steamer courses' and many other special events added to an extremely appealing and successful programme which developed year by year.

The continuous development of the sailing schedule was paralleled by constant work to maintain and improve the ship herself, much of it spearheaded by Chris Smith, the ship's engineer from 1991 to 2006. Paddle boxes were replaced, decks re-laid, a large viewing-hatch created above the engine room, wooden shelters with sliding doors constructed and fabric side screens installed to allow the aft end of the upper deck beneath the awning to be fully enclosed during special events or poor weather and a new companionway leading to the forward saloon was installed. In 1995, the ship's funnel was altered to allow it to be hinged down for passage under Rochester Bridge. The two largest jobs undertaken were the complete re-plating of the bottom during the winter of 1993-94 and the fitting of a new coal-fired boiler in March 2001. The ship, always immaculately turned out, seemed to look better and better with every season that passed.

Needless to say, such a unique ship attracted much media attention and appeared in a number of films and television programmes, including *Our Mutual Friend, Great Expectations, Around the world in 80 Days, Time Team* and *Countryfile.* She played host to a number of well-known personalities such as Sir Harry Secombe, Margaret Thatcher and Prince Edward, was the venue for a well-known annual poetry award and won a number of significant steam and heritage awards herself.

CONTINUING SUCCESS

The continuing success of the Medway operation was due in large measure to the unique and economical manner in which it was managed. For most of her time on the river the ship had only two full-time paid employees, John Megoran and a chief engineer, sometimes supplemented by a paid deckhand or stewardess in high season. All of the other crewing duties were carried out by a small and extremely loyal band of trained volunteers, most of whom also turned their hand to winter refit tasks. Behind the scenes the trustees of the Paddle Steamer *Kingswear Castle* Trust Ltd (which had replaced the previous owning company in 1992) provided vital practical and moral support. This arrangement allowed the ship to make a small profit each season and build up prudent cash reserves and there is no doubt that she could have continued on the Medway for several years to come.

The trustees, however, were aware that the operation of the ship would always be financially fragile and totally dependent on the multi-skilled John Megoran, his engineer and the team of volunteers and were giving careful consideration to securing the ship's long-term future. By happy coincidence, the new General Manager of the Dartmouth Steam Railway & Riverboat Company was also pondering on how well a vintage paddle steamer would fit into his operations and approached the trustees to enquire whether the *Kingswear Castle* might be available. Although initial proposals proved impractical, the two companies remained in close and friendly touch and during 2012 a real possibility arose of the ship returning to the Dart on long-term charter.

While the *Kingswear Castle* carried out her 2012 sailings on the Medway, detailed negotiations continued behind the scenes and, a few days after she ran her final trip on 28th October, it was announced that she would be returning to the Dart in time for the 2013 season on a 15-year renewable charter. Things then moved very quickly. The formal agreement was signed on 15th November and work began on closing the ship up for the long tow back to the Dart. Windows and portholes were boarded up, all moveable deck gear lashed down, temporary bulwarks and decking fitted to the aft well deck and the lower floats removed from the paddle wheels to reduce resistance. The ship left the Medway on 11th December in tow of the local tug *Christine*, ending a remarkable 28 years of operation on the river and bringing a major lump to the throats of her local crew and supporters who would miss her intensely.

RETURN TO THE DART

Tug and tow made good progress and were off the Dorset coast by the morning of 12th December. Unfortunately, a rising wind and sea made it prudent to put into Portland Harbour for shelter where they remained until 18th December when a break

in the weather allowed them to set off again. They arrived at the mouth of the Dart just before dusk that evening to be met by an armada of local boats and several of the Dart river fleet which escorted them upriver. The *Kingswear Castle* was moored to a buoy in mid-river amid a cacophony of boats' sirens and steam locomotive whistles, safely back in the river of her birth after an absence of 45 years.

In January 2013 steam was raised again and the ship began an extensive series of steaming trials on the Dart. John Megoran and Medway engineer Nigel Thomas were on hand to train the new crew and for several weeks the ship was put through every possible evolution. On 7th February she made a successful and historic trial trip to Totnes, the first time she had been there since August 1965. She was then placed on the covered slipway at the company's maintenance yard in Old Mill Creek and, following a detailed and entirely successful Maritime and Coastguard Agency survey, emerged gleaming like a new pin on 12th March.

There is no doubt that the Dartmouth Steam Railway & Riverboat Company has the shipyard facilities, engineering skills and staff to maintain the ship to a very high standard, as well as the infrastructure and advertising expertise to ensure that she is well used. The innovative arrangement between them as commercial operators and the ship's preservationist owners would seem to ensure her future for many years to come, and one can only admire John Megoran and the Trustees for their long-sightedness in finalising the charter agreement.

After further steaming trials, the *Kingswear Castle* took a full load of company employees and their families out for a trip on 24th March and re-entered public service on Good Friday, 29th March. Despite almost arctic temperatures this PSPS benefit cruise, complete with connecting 'Paddle Steamer Express' steam train from Paignton, was a huge success.

For the rest of the season, the *Kingswear Castle* was in service for five days each week. She operated at least three river cruises each day, at midday, 14.00 and 15.15, with an additional 10.30 departure on certain days. These trips took her down to the harbour mouth, passing between the picturesque Dartmouth and Kingswear Castles, before returning upstream past Dartmouth, the Britannia Royal Naval College, Philip & Sons' former Noss shipyard where she was built, Dittisham village and Agatha Christie's former home at Greenway, before turning near the Flat Owers buoy to return to Dartmouth. On several days each month she also offered the stunningly beautiful return trip to Totnes, with the option to make either leg of the journey by bus and steam train as part of a 'Round Robin' ticket and there were even special evening picnic cruises. It is anticipated that a very similar programme will be offered in 2014. The ship has been widely and imaginatively marketed and a great deal of local excitement and goodwill has been generated by her return to Devon.

To sail on board Britain's last coal-fired paddle steamer on the river for which she was designed is a rare delight. Her new crew have fallen in love with her already and take a fierce pride in her appearance. Paintwork and varnish glimmers, highly polished brass and engraved windows sparkle and the only sound is the rhythmic thump of the paddle floats striking the water and the

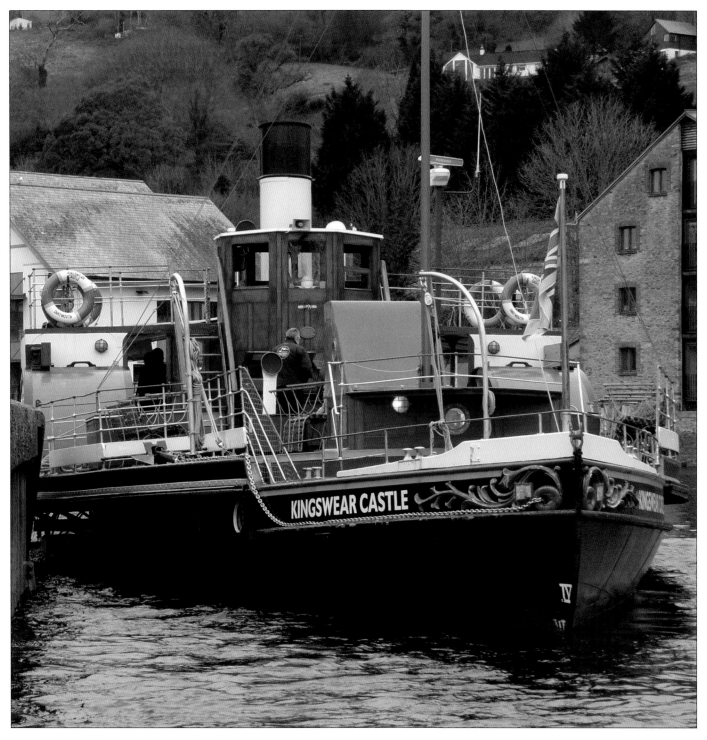

Alongside the Steamer Quay at Totnes on 7th February 2013, on the occasion of her historic first visit to the town since August 1965. The steamer was successfully canted using ropes before returning downstream. *(Richard Clammer)*

occasional blast from her steam whistle. She would be a hugely significant part of our maritime heritage wherever she was located; but placed back in her proper historical context on the Dart her importance is increased manyfold. A trip on board is not to be missed.

Further details of the Kingswear Castle's operation, fares, etc. may

be obtained from:

www.paddlesteamerkc.co.uk
www.dartmouthrailriver.co.uk
www.kingswearcastle.co.uk

A book, "Paddle Steamer Kingswear Castle and Steamers of the River Dart" by Richard Clammer & Alan Kittridge, tells the full story of the ship and her predecessors on the river.

7 The wonderful miniature liners of Istanbul City Lines
by William Mayes

The first recorded regular sailings on the Bosphorus began in 1839 with the Ottoman ship *Mesir-I Bahri* carrying both passengers and cargo. Four years later, the first independent company (actually funded from the Sultan's private fortune) was formed and by 1848 was operating 15 ships in and around Constantinople, and in the Bosphorus. The company went through various incarnations during the later years of the 19th century, but one common feature of many of the ships was that they were built in England. The first steamers, all paddlers, were built by John Robert White of East Cowes, a yard that delivered 15 vessels between 1852 and 1860. Maudsley of London provided the next ten passenger ships including, more interestingly, the first roll-on roll-off vessels, the *Suhulet* and *Sahilbent* in 1870. Initially they were used for the carriage of handcarts and horse-drawn vehicles, but in later years they were quite capable of carrying trucks and cars. Remarkably, the former of this pair survived until taken out of service in 1958, being broken up three years later. Long lives have been a feature of many of the ships

Four small steamers, in reality little more than launches, were built in England in 1872 and shipped out in parts to be finally assembled in the dockyard at Haskoy (now in central Istanbul) of what had become Sirket-I Hayriye. Other companies also operated in the Bosphorus and Halic (Golden Horn), but these were all brought together in 1945 under the name Sehir Hatlari.

The final British-built ships were a series of nine elegant steam-powered vessels delivered by Fairfields in 1960 and 1961, the last three of which survived in service until 2004. One still survives after conversion for use as a boutique hotel at Mudanya, north of Bursa. Subsequently, most of the City Lines ships have been built locally in what is now Greater Istanbul. Most recently five new conventional ships were built at Tuzla, just a few miles to the south of Istanbul. Interestingly, the ferry users were asked what they wanted and the response was basically, more of the same, so the first new ships for almost 20 years are easily recognisable as a development from what went before.

Istanbul City Lines (Sehir Hatlari) was, until March 2005, part of the Turkish Maritime Administration, but as that group wound down and parts of it were sold off, control passed to the Greater Istanbul Municipality who merged the operation into its existing IDO (Istanbul Sea Buses) fast ferry business. When it was eventually decided to privatise IDO, City Lines was largely extracted from the group in 2010 (although the previous City Lines car ferry routes remained with IDO) and was retained by the Municipality as a separate company, resurrecting the name

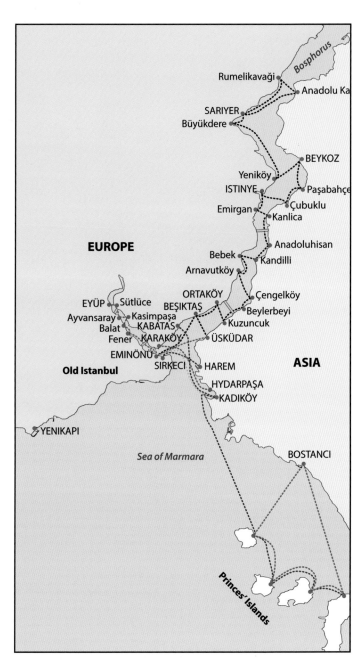

Sehir Hatlari.

The company currently operates 33 ships on 16 routes, but the Marmaray project to extend the Metro system under the Bosphorus to Asia, still running many years late, is likely to have a very serious impact on the ferries when it opens on 29th October 2013, the 90th anniversary of the founding of the Turkish Republic, and may force the closure of several routes when the network becomes fully operational in 2015.

Completed in 1915 by Fairfields, the **Halas** was pressed into service by the Royal Navy as the despatch steamer HMS **Waterwitch** and actually served at Gallipoli. She entered service in Istanbul in 1923 and continued to ply her Bosphorus routes until the mid-1980s. After a period of lay-up she was converted for use as a luxury cruise ship and is still in service.

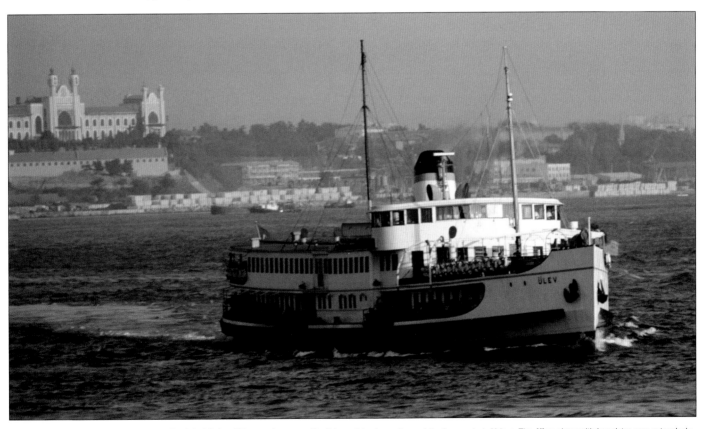

In 1938 a pair of sister ships was delivered by Atlas Werke of Bremen for use on the Princes Islands service and the long route to Yalova. The **Ülev**, along with her sister, was extensively modernised in 1964 and remained in service until sold for scrap in 1990.

In 1948 and 1949 the Schiedam Shipyard in the Netherlands delivered a series of six ships. All were initially coal-fired, but two of the vessels were later converted to burn oil. The **Haydarpasa** was the fifth ship in this class and survived until 1985, when she was sold for breaking.

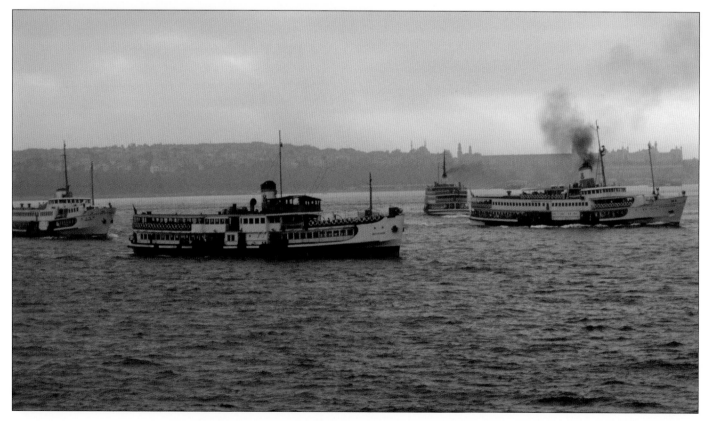

This picture shows a busy scene in 1981 with the **Buyukdere** occupying centre stage. She was a sister to the **Haydarpasa** and the lead ship of the sextet. Converted to oil burning in later life, she remained in service until sold for breaking in 1991. She was outlived by two of her sisters.

Left: William Denny and Brothers at Dumbarton built the **Fenerbahce** and **Dolmabahce**, in 1952. She was one of a pair of ships that were used on the longer routes into the Sea of Marmara and remained in service until 2008, following which she became an exhibit at the Rahmi M Koc Museum at Haskoy, on the Golden Horn.

Above: The **Burgaz** was the final member of a trio of ships delivered in 1912 by Ateliers et Chantiers de Provence of Marie de Port de Bouc in France. Her sisters were scrapped in the 1960s, but the **Burgaz** had a major refit and modernisation in 1969 and continued in service until 1988..

The 'Bahce' class were high-speed ships (18 knots) designed for the long route to Yalova. Cantieri Navali di Taranto in Italy built the **Pasabahce** in 1952. She served her passengers well until withdrawn in 2010 and is believed now to be the subject of a preservation project.

The **Beykoz** was one of a trio of ships built between 1957 and 1962 by the company's own shipyard at Haskoy on the Golden Horn. These vessels were powered by Fiat engines and although her sisters eventually went to Izmir, she continued to operate in Istanbul until the late 1990s.

With a fast-growing population Istanbul needed new and larger ships. Fairfield Shipbuilding and Engineering delivered nine of what were probably the best ships ever to serve Istanbul. The **Pendik** was the third ship of this steam-powered class and operated from 1960 until sold for scrap in 1993.

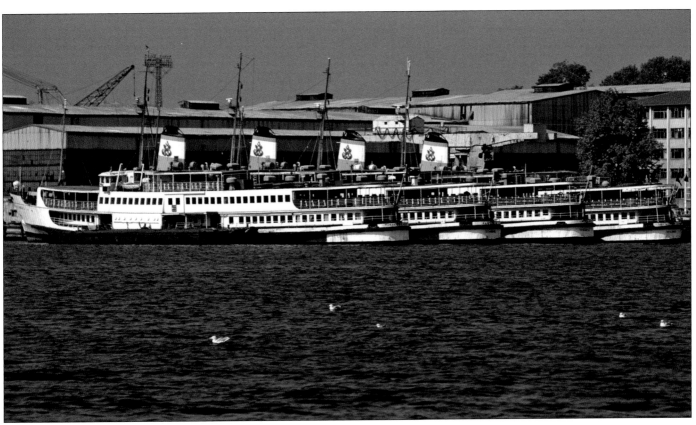

This 2004 photograph shows the last four of the Fairfield steamers laid up after completing their last summer on the Bosphorus. There were projects to use several ships for other purposes, but only one, the **Turan Emeksiz**, seems to have survived and she is now a boutique hotel at Mudanya.

As with most of the large ships, summer passenger capacity of the **Maltepe** and her sister, the **Suadiye**, was 2,100. This duo was built by the Istinye Shipyard, on the Bosphorus in 1962. The **Suadiye** was severely damaged by fire in about 2007 but the **Maltepe** survived until withdrawn from service in 2010.

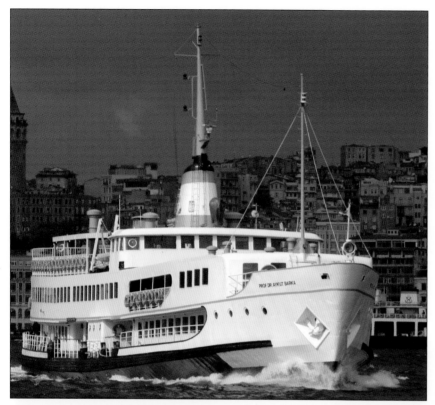

In 1973 three ships were completed and delivered to the company. Built in Istanbul, the **Prof. Dr. Aykut Barka** was delivered as the **Sedefadasi** and served under that name until renamed in 2002 in honour of the late professor of earthquake science at the University of Istanbul. She is still in service.

The **Sehit Mustafa Aydogdu** was the last ship in a batch of ten built on the Golden Horn as First Generation Ships of the Modernisation Programme. The ten ships were delivered between 1976 and 1981 and can be distinguished from the Second Generation ships by the position of the lifeboats, below and in front of the bridge.

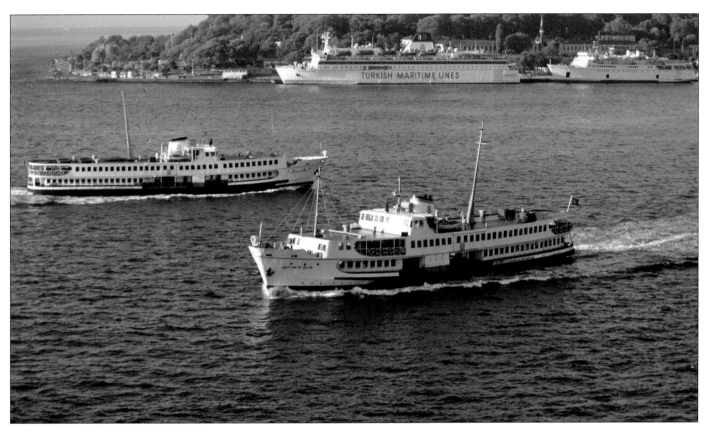

Two of the Second Generation ships are the **Sehit Metin Sulus** (1986) and, in the background the **Nurettin Alpdogan** (1985). The latter is one of just two of this batch of eight ships, which have a fully enclosed forward mid-deck. Of the 18 similar ships in the two series, built between 1976 and 1987, 17 remain in service.

The largest of the Istanbul ferries are used on the busiest routes during the morning and evening peak periods, but during other times these duties are performed by smaller ships. Here is a typical mid-day scene at Eminonou, just ahead of the terminals.

Of the eight so-called Third Generation ships, just the **Zubeyde Hanim** and two of her sisters remain in service in Istanbul. The class were built in three different shipyards and all of those that have been sold on are operating as ferries in other locations in the Istanbul region or in Izmir.

Fourteen small passenger ferries were built on the Golden Horn between 1981 and 1989, in three batches. The **Kumla** was the eighth ship of the last batch of ten and was used on Golden Horn and cross-Bosphorus services until 2008 when all of the ships were withdrawn from service.

They took several years to build, but when delivered in 1989 the *Emin Kul* and her sister became the largest ships to have been built locally for Bosphorus service. These ships usually operate the peak hour services between Eminonu and Kadikoy (on the Asian side of the Bosphorus).

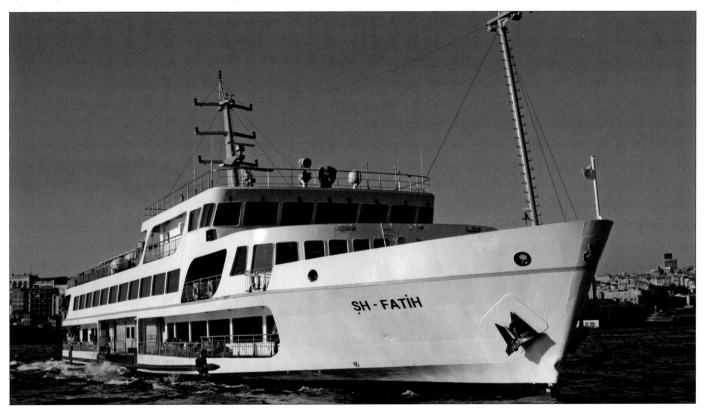

Five new ships were built in the Tuzla shipyard, south of Istanbul and were delivered in late 2008 and early 2009. They retain much of the charm of the older ships, but the main difference is that it is not possible to disembark from the new ships until they are tied up and the doors have been opened. With the older ships it is still common practice for passengers to jump between the ship and quayside while the vessel is still under way.

8 The Sanct Svithun disaster of 1962
by John Bryant

The Hurtigruten (Coastal Express) is rightly called the 'world's most beautiful voyage' and is a great tourist experience but even today its prime purpose remains as serving the needs of communities that live along the coastline line of Norway between Bergen and Kirkenes.

The Second World War had a devastating effect on the route with no fewer than 14 ships being lost during the conflict. The need for new purpose-built tonnage was paramount and on 27th September 1946 a four-ship contract (6 million kroner per ship) was signed with the Italian Cantieri Riuniti dell'Adriatico Shipyard, Ancona for delivery in 1948. There would be one ship for each of the Hurtigruten companies; Det Bergenske Dampskibsselskab (BDS), Det Nordenfjeldske Dampskibsselskab (NFDS), Det Vesteraalens Dampskibsselskab (VDS) and Det Stavangerske Dampskibsselskab (DSD). In the event it would not be until 1949 that the first ship, the *Erling Jarl* for NFDS, would enter service.

Det Stavangerske Dampskibsselskab would be the last of the Hurtigruten companies to receive one of the 'Italia-Båtene'. Named *Sanct Svithun*, after the city's patron saint, the ship was launched at Ancona on 18th May 1950. She was so complete that, having been launched, her first test run was only two hours later, the ship immediately achieving the full specification speed of 17 knots!

ON BOARD

A two-class vessel, the *Sanct Svithun* measured 2,098 gross tons and was 286 feet in length. She had berths for 77 first and 108 second class passengers and held a certificate for 575 persons when on the Coastal Express route. The refrigerated holds had a total capacity of 560 deadweight tonnes or 23,000 cubic feet. Accommodation for both passengers and crew was of a high standard whilst the navigational equipment reflected the massive technological advances made during (and on account of) the Second World War; i.e. gyro-compass, radar, direction-finder, echo-sounder and electric log. Her prime mover was an eight-cylinder 2,500 bhp Fiat diesel, driving a four-bladed Ka-Me-Wa variable pitch propeller and her engine movements could be controlled directly from the bridge or from the engine room. In the end the *Sanct Svithun* was to cost 9.5 million kroner, a significant increase over the original estimate but reflecting the substantial devaluation Norwegian currency had suffered since the end of the war.

The *Sanct Svithun* was handed over on 25th May and arrived at the ship's home port of Stavanger on 7th June, receiving a tremendous welcome. Commanded by Captain Samuel Alshager, she was soon as popular as her predecessor which had been lost in 1943.

Known as the 'ambassador ship', the *Sanct Svithun*'s maiden voyage was from the Festningskaien, Bergen on 8th June 1950. Although identical in layout to her three sisters, the red funnel rings and the DSD motif on the bow made her quite distinctive. Internally, the décor, detailing and atmosphere very much reflected her Stavanger roots; one of her lounges contained a painting of Stavanger Cathedral as well as one by the Italian painter, Lombardo, depicting the *Sanct Svithun* on the slipway at

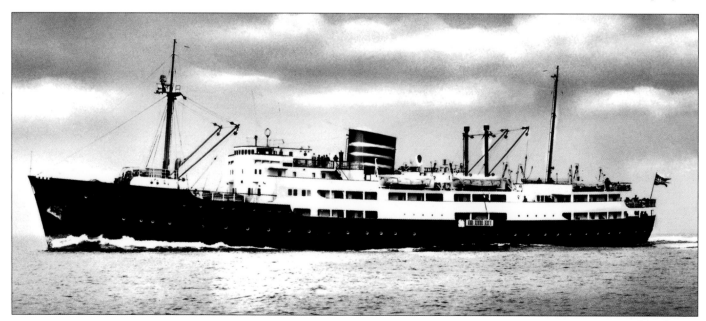

An early 1950s Schrøder postcard view of the ***Sanct Svithun*** off Trondheim. *(Uwe Jakob Collection)*

Ancona, almost ready for launching.

In 1956 Captain Alshager relinquished command and Captain John Andreas Klevland became her new Master. Five years later in February 1961, the *Sanct Svithun* had a thorough refit at the Rosenberg Mek Shipyard in Stavanger in order to bring the ship into line with the new classification requirements in the light of the fire aboard her sister vessel, *Erling Jarl*. The main deck accommodation was refurbished using improved fire resistant materials and new emergency exits were provided. As a result she now measured 2,172 gross tons.

The Hurtigruten, throughout its 120 year long history, has had an outstanding safety record, the standard of seamanship and maintenance of the vessels that operate is of a high order and so tragedies involving the loss of vessels and lives are rare.

OCTOBER 1962

The events of the night of Sunday 21st October 1962 have not been forgotten in Norway, as even today some 50 years later an element of mystery still surrounds what happened out on the Folla on board the DSD flagship, *Sanct Svithun.*

At lunchtime the *Sanct Svithun* had sailed from Trondheim for Rørvik (in the Nord-Trøndelag municipality of Vikna) where she was scheduled to call around 21.00. The wind was in the southwest with a swell rolling in from the Atlantic and there were reports of strong gales and bad weather on this leg of the Coastal Express but up on the bridge the experienced Captain Klevland, on his last trip before retirement, did not appear to be unduly concerned. A total of 89 persons were on board; 40 passengers, two postal workers and 47 crew.

At 21.55 the Rørvik harbourmaster received a radio message from the *Sanct Svithun* that the ship was aground between Allgarden and Gjæslingen, in the main shipping channel, some 12 nautical miles southwest of Rørvik. The *Ragnvald Jarl*, which the *Sanct Svithun* would normally meet at Rørvik, immediately set out for the reported position, and on reaching it sent up a series of distress flares. With all her lights on, the ship should have been visible to any other ship in the vicinity. In radio contact, both ships' Masters were rather puzzled as neither of them could see the flares from each other's vessel.

At 22.45 all radio contact with *Sanct Svithun* was suddenly lost. The final message from Captain Klevland was to the effect that the ship was afloat again but taking in water. At 02.00 the mystery deepened further when a ship's lifeboat came ashore at the Nordøyan lighthouse, some 15 miles west of *Sanct Svithun*'s reported position, its occupants convinced that they had landed at Grinna lighthouse, near Gjæslingen. A second lifeboat then came ashore at Nordøyan, making a total of 30 survivors on the islet. The local steamer, *Vikna*, was sent from Rørvik to collect them.

As soon as it was light, small boats, helicopters and light aircraft joined in the search for any survivors; 17 more were rescued, but sadly 35 bodies were also recovered. The total of dead was later to rise to 42. Among those missing or dead were Captain Klevland, Karl Tysnes, (pilot/navigator) and Ole Solheim (helmsman). The following day, on Tuesday 23rd October, the local priest, Hilmar Romsøy, held a memorial service at the local church in Rørvik.

SHIP LOCATED

It was not until some 38 hours after the first distress call, around noon on the 23rd, that the *Sanct Svithun* was eventually located, lying in 35 fathoms of water, 3.2 nautical miles from Nordøyan lighthouse, and about 200 metres from the Osken reef. This was no less than 15 nautical miles from the reported position of her grounding and a very long way from the shipping lane used by the Hurtigruten ships.

An inquest into the tragedy was opened in Rørvik on 3rd October attended by survivors from the passengers and crew as well as officials from Det Stavangerske Dampskibsselskab.

From the survivors' accounts it would appear that up to 20.00 on that fateful evening the voyage had been totally uneventful as the ship set off down Trondheimsfjorden, later winding her way through the Stokksundet and out into the less sheltered waters off the Buholmråsa lighthouse. Here the *Sanct Svithun* followed a course of 350 degrees into the Folla, at which time Karl Tysnes took over as duty pilot and 17 year old John Karlsen relieved the helmsman.

Between 20.00 and 20.30 the course steered was 342 degrees, taking *Sanct Svithun* well clear of the Nord-Trøndelag coast. As the *Sanct Svithun* neared the group of rocks known as the Grunnan, the order was given to steer '35 degrees'. The helmsman repeated the command, and altered course from 342 degrees to 335 degrees. At 20.45 the course was altered to 333 degrees so as to give way to an approaching ship, before resuming on 335 degrees. It was customary at that time for pilots to give only the final two numbers of a course alteration unless it involved a change of the 'hundreds' digit.

The ship's navigation systems were in good order. There were two compasses in the wheelhouse and whilst both would tend to err by a couple of degrees after a spell of rolling (the *Sanct Svithun* had a reputation as being a lively sea-boat), conditions that night were not so adverse as to be of any consequence.

Shortly before 21.00 Captain Klevland came up to the bridge and was informed by the pilot that according to the reading on the electronic log there should be a lighthouse up ahead. Visibility was now poor so he asked the pilot to switch to a larger range on the radar screen. At the same time Ole Solheim relieved John Karlsen as helmsman, the latter informing him that the course was '35 degrees'.

At 21.55 the ship ran aground. Down in the engine room the main engine was forced upwards by the impact and the two auxiliary diesels almost immediately seized up. Captain Klevland ordered the evacuation of the ship and No. 2 lifeboat was launched and held alongside so that people could board. A number of passengers standing near the deck rail were reluctant to take to the lifeboat.

INQUEST

At the subsequent inquest it was confirmed that the emergency alarm had been activated and was audible throughout the ship, except in the first class accommodation. Whilst passengers seemed reluctant to abandon ship there was no panic as many believed help was near at hand and the ship appeared to

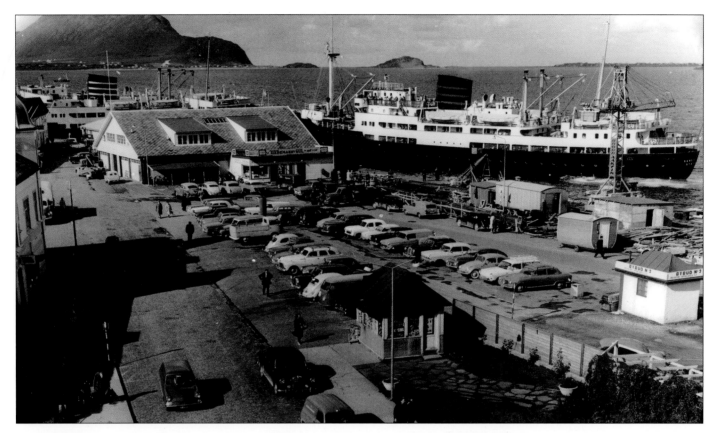

The **Sanct Svithun** is seen arriving at Ålesund, her sister ship, the **Midnatsol** is in the background. *(Hurtigrutemuseet/Hurtigruten ASA)*

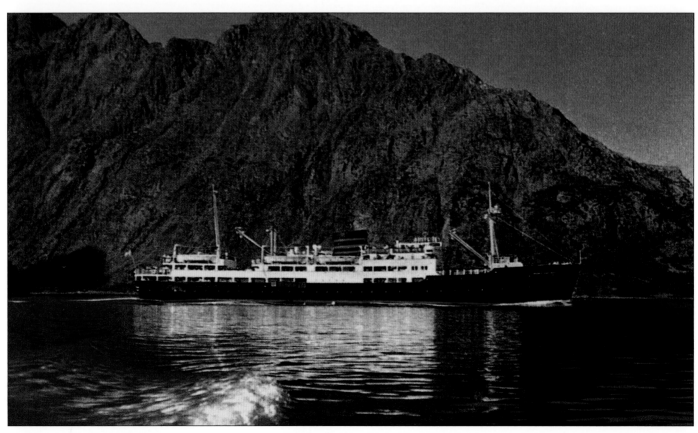

A postcard picture of the **Sanct Svithun** in the Geirangerfjorden. *(Bård Kolltveit Collection)*

be firmly stuck fast. The five lifeboats were all properly equipped and each had room for 36 persons, so even if only the three boats on the starboard side had been launched, there would have been sufficient room on board for all. In general, including the ship's 660 lifejackets, the lifesaving equipment was in good condition.

A large breaker then pushed *Sanct Svithun* off the reef and Captain Klevland gave the order for the port anchor to be lowered so as to prevent the ship from being driven ashore again. Distress flares were again launched and a further radio message transmitted, indicating that the *Sanct Svithun* was afloat again but taking in water.

On deck, the two helmsmen, Karlsen and Solheim bumped into one another, the latter allegedly shouting, 'You gave me the wrong course! It should have been 035 degrees, not 335 degrees!'

The *Sanct Svithun* was now rapidly sinking, listing 35 degrees to starboard with her foredeck almost submerged. At 22.45 the lights went out and the radio became dead. One of the lifeboats was smashed against the side of the ship tipping its occupants into the water. Among the very last to leave the sinking ship was deckhand John Karlsen; caught in the undertow he managed to resurface underneath a life raft and was able to save himself.

As far as the causes of the tragedy are concerned it would appear that the answers lie in the orders given, the actual courses steered and whether these were physically checked by all concerned, particularly at a time when three bridge personnel were being relieved. Nobody therefore was aware how far off course the ship was. The possible misunderstanding between '035 degrees' and '335 degrees' should have been spotted quickly as any decisions after this compounded the situation. Sadly, three of the bridge personnel who could have thrown light on this lost their lives in this tragedy.

Surprisingly too, after Tysnes ordered Karlsen to 'Steer '35 degrees', no one noticed that the nature of the ship's motion had not altered, something which, given a course alteration as much as 60 degrees, would have been obvious. The sea, which would previously have been on the port beam, would then have been on her quarter.

If the ship had continued sailing on 335 degrees on the course steered by Karlsen from 20.30 until 21.00, she would have passed over seven nautical miles south of the skerries around Nordøyan, and out into the safety of the open sea to the west of Vikna. The implication was that sometime after 21.00 there had been a change of course.

Likewise, the lights at Gjæslingen and Nordøyan were not properly checked out, as the former had a continuous white beam whilst the light on the latter shone once every four minutes. Those on the bridge had become somewhat disorientated.

There was also an issue with charts. The *Ragnvald Jarl*, which had set out to search for the *Sanct Svithun*, needed to return to Rørvik for a large-scale chart of that area, mainly because Nordøyan was such a long way from the main shipping channel. It was therefore unlikely that the *Sanct Svithun* would have such a chart. If she had, then those on her bridge might have become aware of the differing characteristics of Gjæslingen and Nordøyan lights.

Afterwards, with all the benefit of hindsight, it was suggested that if the Decca direction-finding system been in place along the Norwegian coast (as it was in neighbouring countries), the tragedy could probably have been averted. A Decca system for the whole Helgeland coast would have cost at that time 1.5 million kroner, a totally insignificant amount when compared with the loss of 42 lives and of a relatively new Hurtigruten ship.

Those who lost their lives on that fateful night on the *Sanct Svithun* are still remembered and over the years a number of memorial services have been held. In 2002 on the 40th anniversary of the disaster a memorial was erected on Nordøyan in memory of all those who died. Sunday 21st October 2012 was a particularly poignant moment, being exactly 50 years to the day since the sinking. Mayor Reinert Eidshaug laid a wreath at the memorial on behalf of the Vikna Port Authority and the local community. Whilst this is likely to be the last official commemoration of the *Sanct Svithun* shipwreck in Vikna for the foreseeable future, the memory is still very strong.

Survivors picked up from the Nordøyan rocks clamber ashore from the fishing boat *Vito*. *(Knut Grindvik Collection)*

One of the *Sanct Svithun*'s lifeboats is manhandled ashore at Rørvik. *(Knut Grindvik Collection)*

The anguish is clear to see as young survivors arrive at Rørvik. *(Knut Grindvik Collection)*

The coffins are laid out in the small church at Rørvik. *(Knut Grindvik Collection)*

9 Battle for the passenger - the impact of the Channel Tunnel
by Richard Kirkman

The year 2014 marks the twentieth anniversary of the opening of the Channel Tunnel from Cheriton to Coquelles. Whilst operator Eurotunnel has never achieved anything like the optimistic traffic levels predicted in the original prospectus, it has nonetheless helped transform the nature of competing cross-channel ferry operations, catalysing quality and service improvements, but prompting route and operator rationalisation. Two decades on, cross-channel carriers have faced significant external challenges whilst adapting their business plans to the massive increase in capacity delivered by the fixed link. This article examines how ferry operators faced up to the challenge of the tunnel and how the numbers of passengers travelling through ports across the English Channel changed in the run up to the opening of the tunnel and its aftermath.

Serious proposals to build a tunnel under the English Channel were first formulated in the early 19th century, with a succession of schemes being promoted but failing to persuade parliamentarians that military interests could be protected. Railway companies frequently promoted these proposals as an extension of their operations in Kent, despite their involvement in the cross-channel shipping trade. Although tunnelling work commenced as early as 1882 - on an alignment similar to that eventually utilised for the Channel Tunnel - the works were abandoned.

Further schemes followed, with construction work starting again in 1974 - only to be stopped when the British government cancelled the project. In 1981 Margaret Thatcher and French President François Mitterrand agreed to set up a working group to look into a privately funded project, and in April 1985 promoters were invited to submit their proposals.

Four bidders were eventually shortlisted. Despite their recent acquisition of Sealink, Sea Containers proposed the 'Channel Expressway', a popular concept of a drive-through twin bore tunnel, but the successful bid comprised a rail-based proposal from the Channel Tunnel Group/France-Manche.

The ferry industry united in opposition under the 'Flexilink' banner and maintained a vigorous campaign of opposition through 1986 and 1987. However government support for the project did not falter and construction work started in 1988, with eleven boring machines being utilised to cut three tunnels (two running tunnels and a service tunnel) through the chalk.

The project included new shuttle terminals at Cheriton and Coquelles; the former supported by completion of the missing section of the M20 between Maidstone and Ashford in 1991. Lobbying from Dover ensured that the Channel Tunnel Bill incorporated powers to continue road improvements onwards to the port, which opened as a dual carriageway extension in 1993.

Breakthrough between French and British bores occurred in October 1990 and the tunnel was formally opened on 6th May 1994. Through freight and shuttle freight services began during the summer of 1994, but Eurostar passenger rail services did not begin until 14th November with passenger shuttle vehicle services following in December.

Although benefitting from a new high speed rail link from Calais to Paris, Eurostar services were forced to utilise a low speed conventional rail route to London Waterloo. It took a further investment of £6.163bn to build the Channel Tunnel Rail Link (now HS1). This opened to Waterloo in 2003 and was extended north to St Pancras International in 2007, involving substantial tunnelling under the Thames and in East London, as well as a new terminal. Planned through rail services from across the UK failed to materialise, despite the procurement of bespoke rolling stock, including a fleet of overnight sleeper vehicles.

Ferry operators had plenty of time to consider their counter-strategy in the near decade from the announcement that the project would go ahead up to the opening of the tunnel. The industry was already familiar with the need to adapt and change and drive business through the exploitation of, for example, tax free sales opportunities. So how did their strategies develop through this challenge to the short sea and Western Channel markets?

The short sea battle

Soon after the July 1985 Channel Tunnel announcement, Townsend Thoresen revealed their plans to counter this threat with an order for two £46m 'Chunnel Beater' vessels - *Pride of Dover* and *Pride of Calais'* - bringing substantially increased capacity compared to their existing fleet. This optimistic response belied financial instability within the parent European Ferries Group, and in July 1986 P&O took a controlling interest in the operation, leading to a formal takeover in December that year.

The arrival of the new vessels was more low-key than anticipated following the tragic loss of the *Herald of Free Enterprise* at Zeebrugge on 6 March 1987. The Townsend Thoresen identity was no longer sustainable, presenting the opportunity for the launch of P&O European Ferries in October 1987.

As construction of the tunnel gathered pace, P&O European Ferries developed its response. First it tackled crew productivity, taking the hit of the interruption to business during the prolonged and bitter crew strike of 1988. Having resolved this issue the

Right: A dramatic mid Channel view of Stena Sealink Line's **Fantasia** with her distinctive dome prominent. Converted to multi purpose usage from a Bulgarian ro-ro freighter in 1989/90, the stability sponsons fitted to the side of the ship are clearly visible. Very much a belated response to the forthcoming opening of the tunnel and P&O European Ferries investment, the conversion was part of the very limited fleet investment made by Sea Containers during their ownership of Sealink. *(FotoFlite)*

Shakespeare Cliff was the site of early attempts to build a cross-channel fixed link and the 1974 access adit. Spoil from the Channel Tunnel works was used to extend the foreshore between Shakespeare Cliff and Abbot's Cliff and provide a construction platform, seen here looking west in August 1990. Work has just begun on constructing the spoil lagoon at the top left of the picture. The area is today known as Samphire Hoe. *(Richard Kirkman)*

The main English construction site and service tunnel access lay alongside the South Eastern Railway's Folkestone - Dover route, seen here disappearing into Shakespeare Cliff tunnel. The gantry cranes transferred concrete segments arriving by the trainload from the Isle of Grain to stockpiles, prior to being taken to site by narrow gauge railway, which was also used to bring out spoil. At the peak of construction some 7,500 tonnes of material were brought in daily. *(Richard Kirkman)*

company moved on to a strategic perspective. The tunnel's primary proposition would enhance focus on the shortest sea crossing by offering faster crossing times and frequent services. But facilities would be limited, prompting Sales & Marketing Director Brian Langford memorably to describe them as restricted to 'a Loo and a light bulb'. The answer was clear; P&O European Ferries would consolidate short sea services at Dover and offer slick, frequent, high quality competition to the tunnel. Accordingly, services to Zeebrugge were withdrawn at the start of 1992 - although RMT continued to offer a service to Ostend - and closure of the Boulogne route followed a year later.

Meanwhile substantial fleet investment continued, with the stretching of the *Pride of Kent* the refurbishment of the *Pride of Bruges* and investment in four new freighters – the fourth destined to become the *Pride of Burgundy*. Completion of this £235m investment programme saw the company introduce a five-ship 45-minute frequency operation a year before the tunnel was due to open. With ships constantly loading in each port and check-in time reduced to 20 minutes, the company laid down the gauntlet of slick intensive operation. Building on the group's cruising heritage, P&O European Ferries raised on-board standards, creating premium 'Club Class' and promoting the whole package under the marketing slogan 'Why sail across when you can cruise across?'

Investment at sea was matched by port authorities, with both Dover and Calais adding link spans to facilitate the rapid and efficient transit of passenger and vehicles through their facilities.

The strategic contrast between P&O and other operators on the short sea routes was stark.

Privatisation of British Rail's Sealink operation in 1984 transferred the conglomerate of ships, routes and ports to Bermuda based Sea Containers. The new owner's initial plans were clouded in confusion, whilst they simultaneously prepared their plans to tender for the fixed link. The anticipated investment in new conventional tonnage did not materialise, with only modest upgrades to the fleet on the short sea routes. A fall out with Belgian Regie voor Maritiem Transport saw the British share in the historic partnership between Dover and Ostend transfer to Townsend Thoresen on a 7 year deal in 1986. In the same year Sea Containers acquired Hoverspeed's hovercraft operations and also made a failed attempt to take over the French SNCF operations.

Converted freighters *Fiesta* and *Fantasia* entered service in 1990 just as the operation was sold to Stena Line, following a fiercely resisted takeover battle. Sea Containers retained Hoverspeed, but Sealink Stena Line now found itself part of the world's largest ferry operation.

The new management took their established Scandinavian approach to the passenger experience and sought to boost on board spend. But this strategy back-fired, resulting in the cost cutting 'Operation Benchmark'. In contrast to P&O, the Sea Containers and Stena approaches lacked clarity of vision and introduced a succession of inappropriate vessels to the intensive short sea operation, typified by the operationally challenging *Stena Invicta*.

Worse followed as Stena's attempted imposition of consistent products across the Anglo-French fleet was resisted by partner Sealink SNAT. Eventually the partnership was dissolved with SeaFrance emerging as an independent French operator, quickly making its mark by prompting a price war to gain market share.

Proposals for a merger between P&O and Stena Line were formulated in 1996 - shortly after the tunnel opened - and the merger (on a 60:40 ownership split) was approved by the authorities, permitting the start of joint operation in 1998. P&O contributed 5 RoRo vessels and 3 freighters to the combined operation, with Stena Line offering 3 RoRo vessels and a fast craft (plus 2 RoRo vessels on the Newhaven - Dieppe route).

The new operation rebranded itself under the P&O Stena Line banner and achieved significant cost efficiencies, but in 2002 P&O bought out the Stena interest and the service reverted to the P&O Ferries brand.

Niche operators on the short sea faced the tunnel challenge with the disadvantage of small market share.

Hoverspeed already offered a fast crossing by ageing hovercraft on the Dover-Calais/Boulogne routes and this was supplemented by the addition of Incat catamarans from 1991; these could offer speed, but not necessarily comfort, on the crossing. The vacuum created by Stena's withdrawal from Folkestone was filled by a further Hoverspeed SeaCat service, but as with their approach to the former Sealink operation Sea Containers failed to provide consistency, deploying the SeaCat fleet across a number of routes - including Portsmouth-Cherbourg - and external charters. The hovercraft survived until 2000 - when the Folkestone route was closed - with a SeaCat service lingering between Dover and Calais until 2005.

SeaFrance started operations with a three ship fleet in 1996 utilising the *SeaFrance Renoir*, *SeaFrance Cezanne* and *SeaFrance Monet*, being supplemented by the '*SeaFrance Manet*' the following year. The aggressive gaining of market share prompted the acquisition of new tonnage in the form of the *SeaFrance Rodin* in 2001 and *SeaFrance Berlioz* in 2006, giving the capability of up to a six ship operation

The Belgian RMT route rebranded as Oostende-Dover Line in 1991 and, following investment at the Belgian port, introduced the *Prins Filip* a year later. As P&O increased focus on the short sea route the marketing relationship between the two parties was terminated in 1992 and RMT brokered a new deal with Sally Line resulting in the transfer of services – including the Jetfoil - to Ramsgate, where port facilities were expanded.

Sally Line had developed their business with a succession of secondhand vessels on the Ramsgate - Dunkirk route, culminating in the *Sally Star*. However the opening of the tunnel hit the operation hard. A joint venture with Holyman Group saw a brief catamaran service introduced to Ostend in 1997, utilising the *Holyman Diamanté* and *Holyman Rapide*, before the latter were acquired by Hoverspeed and transferred to Dover.

Services between Sheerness and Vlissingen grew with the arrival of new builds *Olau Hollandia* and *Olau Britannia* in 1989-90. The company appeared set to face the challenge of the tunnel, but deteriorating relationships with trade unions led to the new vessels being chartered at beneficial rates to P&O European Ferries for the Portsmouth-Le Havre route. The route closed in 1996, after a failed attempt to restart by Ferrylink Ferries.

Chunnel beaters. The clear strategic focus of P&O European Ferries is epitomised by the flagship investment in the **Pride of Dover** and **Pride of Calais**, which provided two decades of high quality service on the Dover Straits. The full £235m fleet programme was completed in time to permit operation of a full 'Channel Shuttle' service a year before the tunnel opened. *(FotoFlite)*

The English terminal at Folkestone lies inland from the main construction activity at Shakespeare Cliff, seen here in August 1990. The M20 lies south of the workings and the vehicle access ramps at the eastern end of the site are beginning to take shape. *(Richard Kirkman)*

The M20/A20 roundabout is clearly visible as construction works scar the landscape. Shuttle services exiting the tunnel would eventually travel along the southern perimeter of the site before looping round back to the terminal facilities. The eventual road access to the terminal lies further east, catching the motorway traffic before the longer drive on to Dover or though the town of Folkestone. *(Richard Kirkman)*

Everyone faced the problem of declining fares. A peak season short sea crossing was typically around £300 in 1994 for a car and occupants. Ten years later competition had forced this as low as £96 - some 30% below what it had been in 1982.

Western Channel

The historic rail-served link between Newhaven and Dieppe formed the shortest route between London and Paris, and had been jointly operated between Anglo French railway interests. Following privatisation of Sealink the route was taken over by SNCF in 1985, but the operation proved troublesome and the route closed in 1992 following industrial action - only to re-open immediately by Stena Line utilising the *Stena Londoner* (ex *Versailles*) and *Stena Parisien* (ex *Champs Elysees*), chartered from SNCF.

Dieppe's new ferry terminal opened in 1994 and fast craft services were inaugurated with *Stena Lynx 1*, but when SNCF terminated the charters to redeploy their vessels on the new Dover - Calais service, Stena was forced to transfer the *Stena Antrim* and *Stena Lynx III*' in 1997. A steady decline and years of unprofitability could not be arrested and the route survived less than a year under the P&O Stena Line banner. Even then Hoverspeed attempted to revive the route in 1999, but the years of a serious passenger operation were long gone.

Brittany Ferries rose from a freight only operation between Roscoff and Plymouth to become the dominant operator on the Western Channel. The company gained its foothold by utilising an expanding fleet of second hand vessels, developing a comprehensive route structure backed a growing package holiday business. An ambitious programme of investment in a purpose built or converted fleet began with '*Bretagne*' in 1989, followed by *Barfleur* (1991), *Normandie* (1992), *Val de Loire* (1993), *Pont-Aven* (2004) and *Armorique* (2008). Each successive investment raised the bar in on board experience, making it increasingly difficult for others to compete.

This investment was predicated on the premise that passengers would pay a premium to travel on longer, higher quality services, where the passage time could be offset against long overland journeys, particularly when travelling to the traditional holiday areas of France - a market which Brittany Ferries did much to promote.

P&O's Western Channel services arose from the takeover of P&O's Southampton operations by Townsend Thoresen, a transfer to Portsmouth as home port, and P&O's reverse absorption of Townsend Thoresen. Routes to Le Havre and Cherbourg developed with transferred tonnage from other routes, with the clumsy stretching of the 'Super Vikings' providing freight capacity but doing little to enhance passenger facilities.

Contrasting with Brittany Ferries and their own short sea approach, P&O's strategy was predicated on low capital investment, with the company choosing in 1994 to charter the two Olau twins – rebadged as *Pride of Portsmouth* and *Pride of Le Havre* – and the chartered *Pride of Bilbao* on a newly opened route from Portsmouth to Bilbao. These dramatically improved on board facilities, driving passenger spend and delivering a substantial increase in volume and quality of overnight cabin accommodation. But they were secured at heavy cost, just as the charter market peaked prior to the opening of the tunnel.

Stena Line's foray into the western channel was short lived. The 'Stena Normandy' re-opened the Southampton – Cherbourg route in 1992, but a one vessel operation could not survive the intense price war as the tunnel opened and the service closed in 1996.

As the passenger market peaked at the turn of the millennium, the price competition from excess capacity on short sea routes, coupled with the loss of tax free sales in 1999 and the rise of low cost airlines, added to the pressures on the western channel operations. And with the collapse in fares on the short sea routes, the price differential for Western Channel routes could no longer be sustained, and fares were driven downwards.

P&O's Portsmouth operation had been free-standing since the creation of P&O Stena Line, but with the reversion to a wholly P&O-owned operation on the short sea these operational restrictions were lifted and the Dover company was able to exert it's influence on the company's wider activities. Cost savings were made by re-integrating the services and creating a fleet-wide shipboard theme consistent with the Dover operation. This only emphasised the gulf in quality with the newer, more market-orientated Brittany Ferries fleet.

P&O's review of these loss-making operations considered radical options, including replacement, cheaper tonnage, a joint venture with Brittany Ferries and, when that floundered, a transfer of services to their competitor. This was vetoed by the Monopolies and Mergers Commission, resulting in the closure of the P&O's Le Havre, Caen and Cherbourg links in 2004.

External forces

As the protagonists shaped up to fight for their share of the cross-channel market, a series of external forces lined up to challenge their ambitions.

The tunnel had opened at a time of comparative weakness of the pound against European currencies. As the decade progressed the currency gradually strengthened, peaking in summer 2000 in parallel with growth in the cross channel market. In the following decade there were big falls in 2003 and a prolonged drop between 2008 and 2009, reaching almost parity against the Euro at the end of 2009.

From 1993 the EU phased in an open skies regime, completing airline deregulation in 1997, giving carriers from one EU country the right to operate scheduled services between other EU states. This prompted growth of low cost airlines leading to expanded route structures and a dramatic lowering of fares. Ryanair alone ordered 300 Boeing 737 aircraft between 1998 and 2003 and by the end of that year flew 127 routes, of which 60 had opened in the previous 12 months.

The abolition of duty-free was agreed in 1991 on the grounds that cut-price sales to cross-border travellers within the EU was anomalous in a single market, but the industry was granted an extra six and a half years to adjust. The decision was upheld in 1989 despite strong lobbying by Britain, Germany and France. So from 30 June 1989 the sale at sea of duty-free alcohol, cigarettes and other consumer goods ended within the European Union,

An unkempt looking *Fiesta* passes her Sealink sister *Fantasia* in her Sealink British Ferries livery. The lack of consistency in branding demonstrates the difficulties inherent in the blend of French and British operation of the Sealink product. Operation under Sea Containers' control was short lived and the run up to the opening of the tunnel saw successor Stena Line grappling with financial difficulties. *(FotoFlite)*

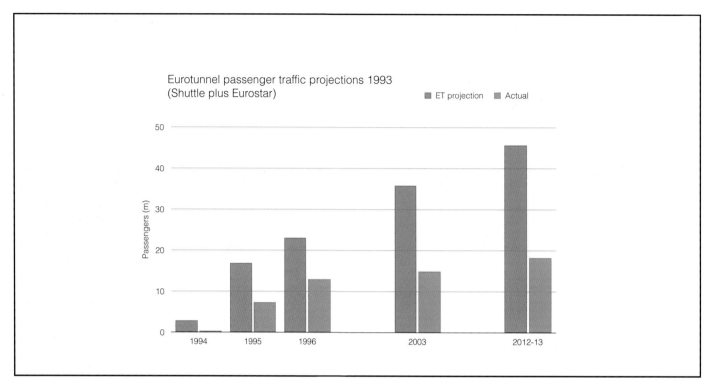

Eurotunnel passenger traffic projections 1993
(Shuttle plus Eurostar)

becoming subject to the VAT and excise duties of the country where the journey had started.

At a stroke the rationale behind a cheap duty free 'booze cruise' was abolished and a substantial market and income source was lost to the ferry industry.

So in addition to fighting each other for market share, the tunnel and ferry operators faced serious external threats to their business. How did each fare after the tunnel opened?

Channel tunnel business case benefits were never realised.

Eventual construction costs turned out to be 80% over budget - £4.65bn at 1985 prices - and traffic projections proved wildly optimistic. Eurotunnel employed specialist consultants to compile traffic projections, seeing the whole cross-channel market - including air - as their target. But their predictions fell well short of reality.

The tunnel launched services at a difficult time, as the pound fell against European currencies in 1993 and 1994. As might be expected, shuttle traffic grew dramatically in the first two years of

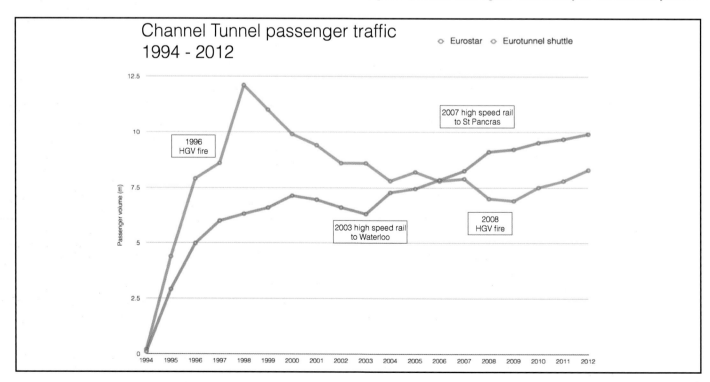

Channel Tunnel passenger traffic
1994 - 2012

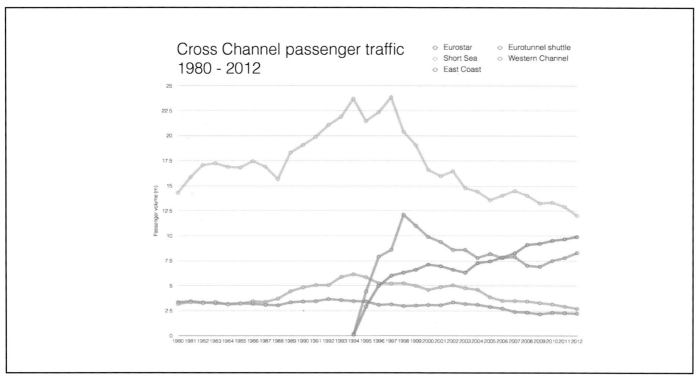

operation as the service expanded. But this growth was constrained after fire broke out on an HGV shuttle wagon in the tunnel on 18 November 1996, and it took a full 6 months for services to return to normal. Combined shuttle and Eurostar passenger traffic peaked in 1998 at 18.4m, falling back to 14.9m in 2003, with gradual recovery thereafter fuelled primarily by Eurostar services, with noticeable increases following the opening of the Channel Tunnel Rail Link to Waterloo in 2003 and the full service to St Pancras International in 2007.

The original traffic projections for Eurostar envisaged 15.9m passengers in the first full year of operation; but the reality was a less spectacular 2.92m in 1995, peaking at 7.13m in 2000. Traffic fell between 2000 and 2003. Higher speed rail operations in the UK prompted spurts of growth from 2004 and 2007, with gradual growth thereafter.

After a low point in 1988, short sea ferry volumes grew in the 6 years prior to tunnel opening, experiencing a dip as the tunnel opened and then recovering growth as the tunnel traffic was

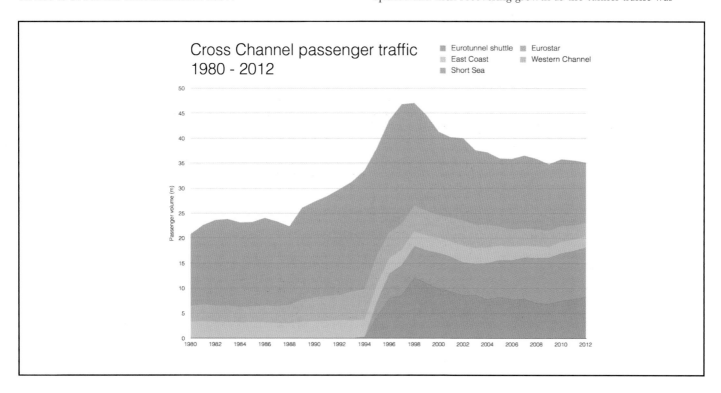

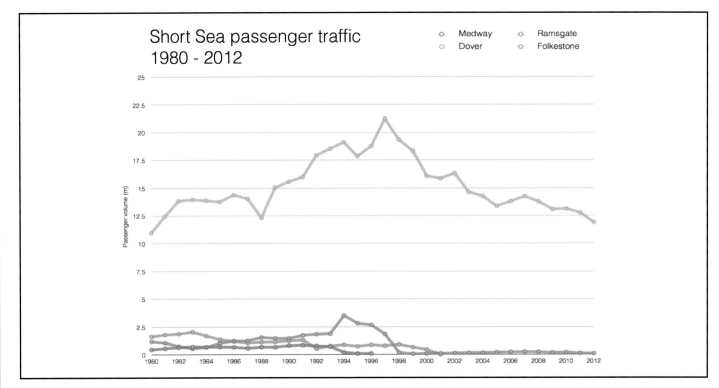

stunted by the fire of 1996. But after the peak of 1997, volumes have gradually declined, and are now consistently below 1980 levels. From the tunnel peak of 1998, shuttle business followed a similar decline to ferry competitors, dropping to a low in 2009, from which a partial recovery has been made.

Western Channel business grew as Brittany Ferries and P&O European Ferries invested in their operations. Volumes peaked in 1994 and exhibited a gradual decline thereafter, falling back to

levels below the 1980s by 2012, albeit with Brittany Ferries enjoying a virtual monopoly by this time.

The cumulative market position demonstrates the surge in ferry and shuttle business through the 1990s peaking in 1999, but falling thereafter. Even Eurostar volumes benefitting from substantial investment in the high speed rail route HS1, failed to stem this overall fall in business.

The short sea market has consistently been dominated by

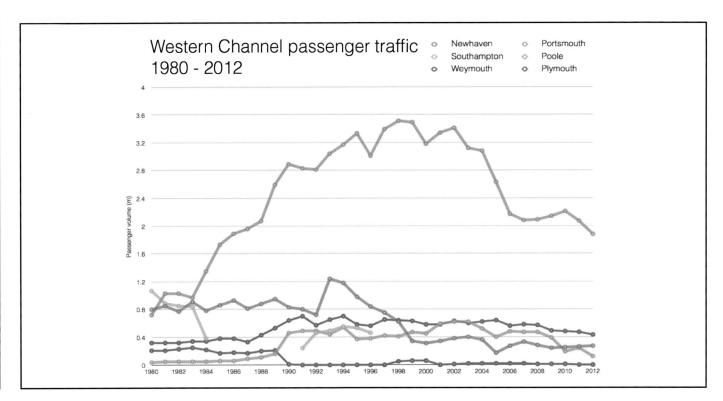

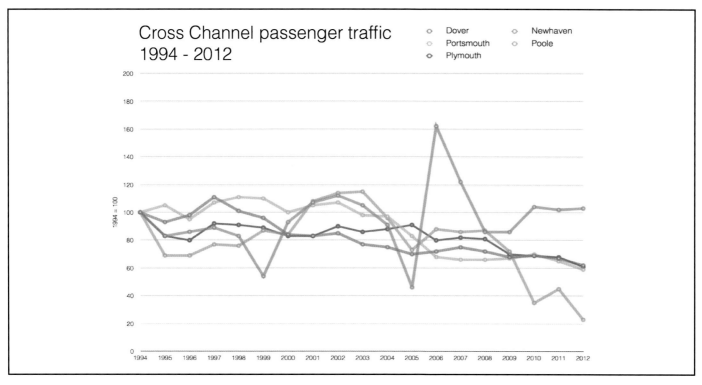

Cross Channel passenger traffic
1994 - 2012

Legend: Dover, Portsmouth, Plymouth, Newhaven, Poole

Dover based operations, with the decline of services from the Medway, Folkestone and Ramsgate reflecting market consolidation. Yet the Dover ferry operations now carry fewer passengers than in the period prior to the pre-tunnel investment. And fares are back to 1990s levels, despite 20 years of inflation.

Further West, Portsmouth has been the dominant port since the transfer of services from Southampton in 1984, with business climbing to peak in 1999, with relatively stable volumes prior to the withdrawal of P&O services and the consequent decline in business falling back below the 2m passenger level in 2012. Southampton's volumes were intermittent after Townsend Thoresen's departure, and Newhaven has suffered a prolonged fall from the peak of 1993. Both Poole and Plymouth benefitted from the Brittany Ferries investment programme, seeing growth through the late 1980s and stable levels of business thereafter, with limited impact from the tunnel. But pressure on Brittany Ferries and the gradual reduction of services took Poole back to levels enjoyed before the expansion programme.

How did each port fare in relative terms? Using 1994 as a base level the demise of Ramsgate and Folkestone is immediately apparent, but other routes weathered the storm and by 2000, no remaining route had lost more than 18% of the pre-tunnel volume. Some further relative improvement followed in the early years of the new millennium, but in recent years the fortunes of Dover, Portsmouth and Plymouth have aligned closely, such that from 2009 to 2012, each ended up 40% down on 1994 traffic levels.

Two decades on, who are the winners and losers from the opening of the Channel Tunnel? As it turned out, the increase in capacity delivered by the opening of the tunnel was only one factor in the market changes that followed. Few industries have witnessed the almost continuous change in route structure,

operators, corporate ownership, capacity and quality as experienced in the cross channel ferry industry since the mid 1980s. The tunnel has equally been stifled by the impact of low cost airlines, fluctuating exchange rates, rising fuel costs, and the loss of tax free sales income. But the influence of the tunnel is seen in the over-provision of capacity that ultimately drove fares downwards. Whilst passengers benefitted from significantly lower prices - coupled with better quality services - this is be balanced against a more restricted choice of routes and operators.

In late 2013 significant passenger operations from Felixstowe, Sheerness, Ramsgate, Folkestone, Zeebrugge, Ostend and Boulogne are a memory, and Olau, Sally Line, Sealink, Stena Line and SeaFrance have gone from the Channel. The long term survivors in the ferry industry are those who committed to the fleet investment necessary to provide the right product in the right market. Both P&O and Brittany Ferries devised and backed visionary strategies based on significant fleet investment that could withstand the battering of competition and external challenge. Whilst profitability and corporate ownership might not have evolved in the ways envisaged, they remain the dominant forces. P&O's stance in the Western Channel lacked capital commitment and was less successful.

From the outset Eurotunnel faced stronger competition than anticipated, and with higher costs and lower revenue than planned was forced to adopt financial restructuring. As the one permanent feature of the market it will always be a key player. But thoughts of exercising options for a second tunnel have long evaporated, and who would have predicted their foray into ferry operations in 2013?

10 Europa 2
by Lynn Houghton

Bubbly Ballast (1,000 bottles of Champagne), Suite-only accommodation and more space per passenger than any other cruise ship afloat; meet the new Hapag Lloyd ship, *Europa 2*.

It is always a privilege to be on the shakedown of a new cruise ship, especially one with a pedigree as impressive as the *Europa 2*. I was able to travel to Southampton and be one of the very first to experience a vessel whose owners claim it is 'the most beautiful at sea'.

The *Europa 2* is a very different proposition from Hapag Lloyd's other, more traditional luxury ship, *Europa*. Clean, modern and relaxed are how the company describe this new offering. It is all about having choice, and plenty of it. Meal times are flexible as is the dress code. It is a bi-lingual cruise with both German and English spoken. According to Douglas Ward, The Berlitz Guide to Cruising, 'Europa' class ships are the best in the world, top in the industry, the crème de la crème. I will be interested to see if I feel the 'wow' factor.

FIRST IMPRESSIONS

My first impression of the *Europa 2* is the vast amount of space (76.5 metres per passenger to be exact); and sheer whiteness of the vessel's interior. Several of the artworks, 890 in total, are also completely white to match the background. I hear some guests using the word 'clinical' as a description, though I think that is far too harsh. What I would say is that the white décor adds to the feeling of space; indeed, when you factor in all the glass and light, the effect is sheer translucence.

But it isn't just the décor that is remarkable, there are the new technological achievements that are part of the *Europa 2* that

stand out. When the drawings were first penned for this vessel in 2006, the plan was for each cabin or suite to have its own stationary PC. Of course, people now require mobility which means tablets and iPhones and docking stations – desk top PCs are pretty much extinct only seven years on.

Construction on the *Europa 2* began on 5th September 2011 in Saint Nazaire, France with the cutting of the steel, a computer-generated laser seared through the 20mm-thick steel on the first section of the ship. Bigger cruise ships had been built in these yards but nothing had been built that was as luxurious as the *Europa 2*.

Housed in the same building, the cabin 'factory' had constructed a 1:1 scale mock-up of the $35m^2$ Verandah Suite and also of the $52m^2$ Spa Suite. The product management team, engineers, electricians, architects and even the head of housekeeping examined and scrutinised the mock-ups. Any corrections on the design of these suites needed to be made at this very early stage, even though continual adjustments would happen as the build went on.

Over the next two years, the planners would continue to look for the right balance between practical and the desirable in building the *Europa 2*. Often the solutions would be dictated by economic factors. Even the wall-to-wall carpeting for the $23,000m^2$ of floor space would be carefully chosen as every additional ton of weight had to be balanced out by six tonnes of ballast.

KEEL LAYING

The keel laying, symbolically an important event, took place on 1st March 2012 when the 400-ton block No. 104 was

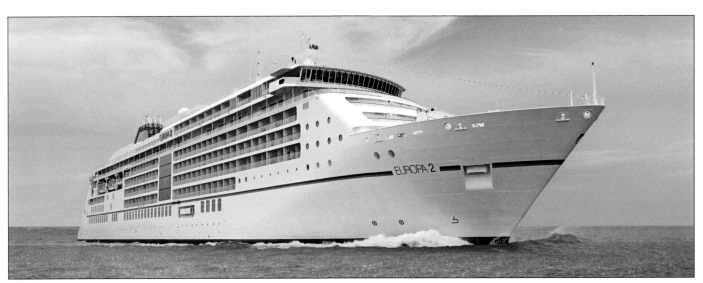

Hapag Lloyd's new ship, the **Europa 2**. *(Hapag Lloyd)*

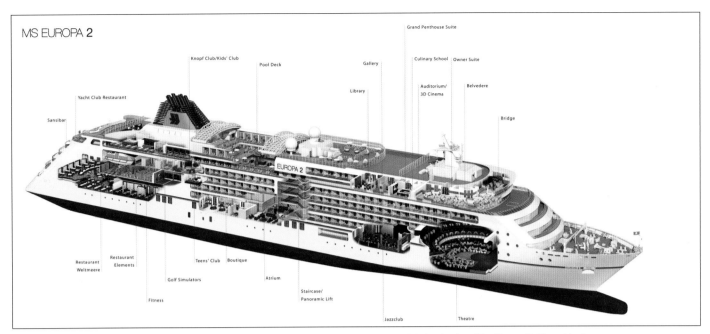

MS EUROPA 2

Grand Penthouse Suite

Knopf Club/Kids' Club
Pool Deck
Gallery
Culinary School   Owner Suite

Yacht Club Restaurant
Library
Auditorium/
3D Cinema
Belvedere

Sansibar
Bridge

EUROPA 2

Restaurant
Weltmeere
Restaurant
Elements
Teens' Club   Boutique
Atrium
Staircase/
Panoramic Lift

Golf Simulators
Fitness
Jazzclub
Theatre

Layout and design drawing of the **Europa 2**. *(Hapag Lloyd)*

Construction in progress in the drydock at Saint Nazaire, France. *(Hapag Lloyd)*

The **Europa 2** being floated out of the drydock. *(Hapag Lloyd)*

ceremoniously lowered. Historically, the keel is the backbone of every ship and the main source of its structural integrity. The hull, which keeps a ship afloat, would now be seen from below. And the bulbous bow, which lays under the water line, will generate a wave that moves around the hull as the ship is moving, reducing drag and conserving energy.

The two stabilisers, with a $14m^2$ fin-shaped area, will have the important task of keeping this large vessel sailing smoothly, whatever the weather conditions, particularly when it is dealing with wind and waves.

The two Azimuth thrusters on the stern are also known as 'mermaid pods'. These Rolls Royce branded propellers have a 360-degree turning radius and will also steer the ship. Because there is no shaft from the engine room going down into the propulsion pods, there is almost no vibration during the cruise. The four propulsion engines produce a total output of 29,000kW, 14,500kW for each propeller (pod) which is the equivalent of 32,600 hp. The engines are at their most efficient with a 75-85 per cent load (using between 4,500 and 5,000kW hours) and 0.65 tonnes of fuel used per kW hour.

Silvio Ple u, Chief Engineer for the *Europa 2*, spoke to me about the new concepts and mechanics being used on this unique ship. With the focus on ecology, he said the *Europa 2* would be the first ship to be equipped with SCR – catalytic converters to reduce nitric oxide emissions. These 'scrubbers' clean the insides of the engines using ammonia. Ultimately, this reduces emissions into the atmosphere in the same way that catalytic converters do on cars.

The *Europa 2* is also the first cruise ship to utilise SRTP (safe return to port) technology – an important new concept. For instance, the ship will now be capable of running on two engines even though there are four. On a typical sailing day, *Europa 2* will normally run on three engines. There are also two fuel tanks in the bow of the ship and two in the stern. If there is a fire in one part of the ship, it is compartmentalised so that only that section

Serenissima Italian Restaurant on the **Europa 2**. *(Hapag Lloyd)*

Terragon French Restaurant on the **Europa 2** specialising in Brasserie style food. *(Hapag Lloyd)*

will be affected. So the ship, in theory, should never be without fuel. The same is true with water-tanks and air-conditioning compressors, two are in the bow area and two in the stern. There is even a standby unit for toilets that will kick in automatically should there be any problem with the vacuum flushing system.

There are two sewage units (prototypes) for the advanced treatment of water. Grey and black water will be collated into the two units and treated, with the water then pumped out clean and ready for use. The other new unit is for treating bio-sludge which is now dried and either incinerated or put into rubbish bags to be taken shoreside. Two osmosis systems provide clean potable water as well as water for cooling the engines.

There is 100 per cent fresh air on board the *Europa 2*, no air is ever re-circulated. A sensor in every suite gauges the CO_2 content and ensures that the air is fresh, with no more than 411 ppm of CO_2. There is even a gap under the door of the toilet to allow air to flow into the room, so that odours cannot leak out.

The retractable roof over the entire pool area weighs a staggering 20,000 tonnes and is one of the most sophisticated at sea, closing in just a few minutes.

Moving from the *Europa*, Captain Akkermann has taken over as Captain of the *Europa 2*. He is very proud of his new 'baby'. Coming from a long tradition of sea captains, 12 generations to be exact, he has been sailing for over 30 years. As there are no gala dinners or Captain's cocktail parties on the *Europa 2* (in order for passengers to have more time to themselves), hopefully, guests will spot him at the theatre or have the chance to speak to him as he walks around the ship. Of course, all on board will still hear the Captain's daily report over the tannoy.

THE HOTEL

The *Europa 2* has a vast reception area on Deck 4 with tall deck heads and a comfortable, expansive seating area covered with velvet embossed fabrics. There is also a low slung bar (with bartenders standing below the passengers). A grand piano is strategically placed in front of the reception desk and two enormous lamps in the seating area nearly reach the top of the ceiling. This ship has clearly been well thought out from conception through to delivery and it shows in the details.

The next obvious feature is that the sea is visible from almost everywhere on the vessel. Even though the inside of this ship looks like a modernist hotel, you never forget that you are at sea.

Initially, you can't help but notice the level of attention given by the staff. Quietly waiting to serve you a glass of champagne or assisting with your luggage, this is the service that Hapag Lloyd has built its reputation on. It is very intuitive, slightly cool, not 'in your face' but every bit as friendly as staff on other ships. Attention to details such as hand-made carpets, strawberries in your suite on arrival and a free mini bar stocked twice a day are all par for the course.

Overall there are eight restaurants and six bars on board the *Europa 2*. There is a theatre with a capacity for 400, a spacious spa and gym that feature muted colours and wood interiors. Fitness is certainly a focus here and goes along nicely with the relaxed vibe of the ship. There is a cookery school which offers cooking lessons from 80 Euros per person though workshops are

The **Europa 2** at sea. *(Hapag Lloyd)*

Elements Asian Fusion Restaurant on the **Europa 2**, *(Hapag Lloyd)*

The Jazz Club on the **Europa 2**. *(Hapag Lloyd)*

The impressive Reception area. *(Hapag Lloyd)*

Pool deck with fully retractable roof. *(Hapag Lloyd)*

Windemeere Restaurant on the **Europa 2**. (Hapag Lloyd)

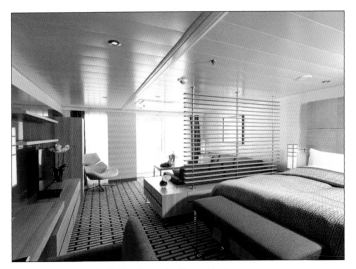

Spa Suite on **Europa 2** with 52 m² veranda. (Hapag Lloyd)

free.

Suites are very spacious and range in size from 28m² to 99m² and include Veranda Suites, Grand Penthouse Suites, Owners Suites and Ocean Suites and each has a balcony.

The Spa Suite was actually my favourite cabin as far as layout was concerned and comes with butler service. The suite is 42m² with a balcony that is 10m² and boasts a living room with t-shaped modular sofa plus a stylish armchair. The living area is separated from the bedroom by open wooden slats. The bed is enormous and unbelievably comfortable. My only feeble complaint is that there are too many different buttons for turning off various lights. A master switch by the door is handy but then it is completely dark and pretty difficult to find the way back to your bed. There is an enormous flat-screen TV as well as espresso machine. A rain shower with steam sauna as well as a whirlpool tub means the bathroom is exceptional. In fact, each level of accommodation has a bathtub and, nearly all, have a window between the bathroom and bedroom. So when you pull up the blinds, again, you have a view of the sea.

Cuisine is also at the forefront of the Hapag Lloyd's 'mission to please'. The Head Chef, Stefan Wilke, spent many months creating the menus for each of the restaurants and, importantly, all dining is included in the price of the cruise. But, take note, wine is not included with meals and there are certainly some very expensive offerings on the wine list.

The breakfast buffet at The Yacht Club on Deck 9 is full of surprises and variety. Guests can have everything from an English fry up, to curry or fancy yoghurts. The Yacht Club is also open for dinner and is a popular option if the weather is warm. Dinner here is also buffet style but includes a pasta bar and grilled meat corner. The Weltmeere (World Seas) restaurant is the main dining room and has a wide selection of dishes.

The Serenissima is the ship's Italian restaurant and specialises in pasta, anti-pasta, fish and meat dishes. The Elements Restaurant focuses on fusion Asian cuisine. Delectable desserts are a feature of The Terragon French Restaurant which also offers traditional brasserie food such as Chateaubriand with Pommes Frites. The Grand Reserve, attached to the Tarragon, focuses on fine wine and French food pairing.

Afternoon tea with cakes and pastries are served in the Belvedere Room on Deck 9 while Sansibar, also on Deck 9, doubles as a dance club/bar at night and breakfast station in the morning. After hours, the Jazz Club is a popular haunt though many guests enjoy hanging out on the pool deck particularly if there is a live band.

The 1,000m² spa encompasses the fitness centre, salon and golf simulator as well as eight treatment rooms. One of these is a private suite with two massage beds and there is also Hammam room. There is a relaxation area with heated loungers, Kniepp step pool, Jacuzzi, Finnish sauna and outdoor deck for relaxing as well. The sports desk staff will assist with booking golf lessons, organising a personal trainer and also booking golf reservations on shore.

Hapag Lloyd have tried their utmost to provide: comfort, wonderful cuisine and a relaxing environment on this, their latest ship. By and large, they have succeeded. Anyone with the opportunity to sail on the *Europa 2* should certainly jump at the chance.

Fact file for the Europa 2

Builder:	STX, France, Saint Nazaire
Completion date:	2013
Flag:	Malta
Length:	225,138 metres (739.44ft)
Breadth:	26.70 metres (87.60ft)
Draught:	6.3 metres
Gross tonnage:	42,830
Propulsion:	Azimuth Thrusters (mermaid pods)
Top speed:	21 knots
Passengers:	516 (maximum)
Crew:	370
Number of Suites:	251

Eastern Dock, Dover *(John Hendy)*

11 The ferry branding game
by George Holland

Branding – it's all around us. Every consumer product and service has a brand and there is much money to be made by those who provide companies and organisations with 'brand solutions'.

Until the early 1960s, the Channel ferry fleets were virtually devoid of any corporate markings on their exteriors. Almost without exception, hulls were either black or dark blue, funnels red or buff. All this was to be shaken up with the emergence of that brave pioneer of the ferry industry, Mr Otto Thoresen. This Norwegian entrepreneur didn't just revolutionise cross-Channel sea travel; in doing so he revolutionised approaches to ferry branding too. The 'Thoresen Vikings' were not only the first drive-through ships to link England with France, they sported a livery that was remarkably different to anything seen before. The garish orange hulls were adorned with the Company name spelt out in white block lettering while the pale green funnels featured the Company emblem; another innovation on the Channel.

A year later, the first British registered drive-through ferry on the Channel was introduced by Townsend Car Ferries. Perhaps inspired by Thoresen's audaciousness, the *Free Enterprise II* sported her operator's name in prominent red block capitals along the forward end of her superstructure (the earlier *Free Enterprise I* followed suit). In addition, an illuminated version of the brand name was also installed on her bridge deck. This somewhat extravagant feature was to also appear on all subsequent 'Free Enterprise' class vessels.

With Townsend and Thoresen having set a trend for displaying corporate markings on vessel exteriors, British Railways underwent a 'rebranding' as British Rail in 1964 and this saw the introduction of that famous transport icon, the white 'double arrow', to the red funnels of the railway-owned fleet. The Design Research Unit was also responsible for BR's 'Rail Alphabet' typeface, which was eventually used from 1972 to depict the 'Sealink' brand logotype in white against the 'Monastral Blue' (deep blue, with a hint of turquoise) hulls of the fleet. The *Hengist* and *Horsa* were the first new BR ships to be delivered in the complete Sealink livery and they demonstrated the advertising potential of displaying the brand name in huge proportions along the sides of the ships themselves. British Rail had established a unified look to its rail and sea services, with 'Monastral Blue' and grey adorning their rolling stock and ferries, along with the double arrow insignia and Rail Alphabet labelling. The grey upperworks were short lived on seagoing vessels, however. Masters complained that that they were dangerous in poor visibility conditions. Masts, nevertheless, remained BR grey.

The now familiar colours of Stena Line made their first appearance at Calais as early as 1965 when their short-lived service from Tilbury opened. The compact and ultra modern *Stena Nordica* featured the same white 'S' insignia on her red funnel (in her particular case a dummy funnel) that is still in use to this day. On her 'cruising white' hull the marketing slogan 'The Londoner' was painted. The Stena 'S' also appeared in a shield-shaped motif on her prow, complete with gold pinstripes either side. It was an ostentatious expression of corporate identity, evoking notions of prestige and pride. Vessels of the former Sealink UK fleet adopted the shield feature in 1996 when the Stena Line brand was relaunched with modifications to the colour scheme and lettering: Navy blue was used instead of gold,

The second of Thoresen's trailblazing 'Viking' series was the **Car Ferry Viking II**. The unfortunate 'Car Ferry' prefix was necessary as there was already a **Viking II** on the Norwegian ship register. *(Ferry Publications Library)*

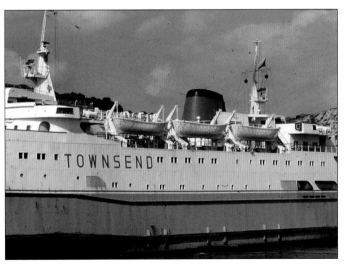

The **Free Enterprise II** of 1965 was the first Townsend ship to feature prominent branding in her livery. The pea green hull, previously seen on **Free Enterprise I**, was said to be inspired by Cunard's liner, **Caronia**. *(John Hendy)*

An aerial view of the **Vortigern**, displaying the Sealink branding introduced for the 1972 season. Note that her masts are grey as opposed to white. The distinctive funnel (a hallmark of BR's naval architects, Don Ripley and Tony Rogan) had the double-arrow signage applied in relief. *(FotoFlite)*

The splendid **Côte d'Azur** is seen on trials off Folkestone having been delivered to SNCF as their new flagship in September 1981. Behind her the **Hengist** is heading for Boulogne. It can seen that the British and French Sealink ships featured very similar colour schemes during this period. *(FotoFlite)*

The **Prins Philippe** is seen wearing the traditional Belgian Marine colours of black hull and buff/yellow funnels and masts. The 'Sealink' lettering was applied in BR's Rail Alphabet font, whilst the stylish RMT monogram made its first appearance on her funnel (in navy and pale blue). Inexplicably her black hull paintwork was lowered one deck after her maiden season, with the lettering being consequently reduced in size too. *(FotoFlite)*

and a modern italic sans serif font replaced the previous block capitals.

During the 1970s the Sealink brand was adopted by BR's Continental partners; France's SNCF, Belgium's RMT, and The Netherlands' SMZ. Now 'The Big Fleet' (a marketing device coined in the 1960s) had a common livery feature. The Sealink brand appeared on various colours of hulls (blue, white, or black), in lettering loosely based on Rail Alphabet. Funnels proudly retained the colours and emblems of their respective countries: RMT devised a clever monogram interlinking their three initials in a tramline style. This was applied to their traditional buff/yellow funnels and was first seen on the new *Prins Philippe* of 1973. SNCF's first italic logotype was designed as early as 1967, but didn't appear on their ferries until 1975. SMZ resisted the temptation to deploy any logo devices until the *Koningin Beatrix* of 1986 which featured a stylised crown emblem on her funnel.

The Townsend Thoresen brand was born back in 1968 through the merger of Townsend and Thoresen Car Ferries. The two companies still existed as self-contained units of the newly formed European Ferries Group. However, for the purposes of marketing, the joint name was utilised. The Townsend Thoresen moniker appeared in white block lettering along the pale green hulls of Dover-based ships, and the orange of the Southampton vessels. A 'TTF' monogram was applied in contrasting hues to the Townsend red and Thoresen pale green funnels. It wasn't until the delivery of the 'European' class vessels of 1975/6 that the Dover-based ships finally conformed to their Southampton counterparts in terms of colour schemes: a protracted process of harmonisation indeed.

By 1984, with vessels at Dover, Southampton (and the former ASN ports of Felixstowe and Cairnryan) all wearing a standardised colour scheme, Townsend Thoresen dispensed with their orange TTF funnel monogram in favour of a much cleaner white on green design: The new 'TT' insignia presented a bold, modern image for the fleet. On the *Free Enterprise IV* and *Free Enterprise V* it was even implemented as an illuminated piece of signage, rather than just painted on. But it was to last just three years due to a totally unforeseen event: the Zeebrugge ferry disaster of March 1987 resulted in scenes of the Townsend Thoresen flagship being broadcast around the world in the worst possible circumstances. The horrifying spectacle of the *Herald of Free Enterprise* lying on her side, half submerged in the North Sea, meant that the TT logo would forever after be associated with that dreadful incident. Within weeks of the catastrophe, the surviving fleet members had their TT funnel markings removed.

European Ferries had been acquired the previous year by the P&O Group, and perhaps it was envisaged that Townsend Thoresen would eventually be rebranded to reflect the change in its ownership. However, if such plans were in the pipeline, the process was, no doubt, hastened by the desire to bury the now tarnished TT brand. The new *Pride of Dover* entered service in June 1987 with a standard Townsend Thoresen orange hull, but her funnel was painted pale blue and featured P&O's venerable billowing flag emblem (originally designed by Wolff Olins). By the time that the *Pride of Calais* was delivered that December, all

The **Spirit of Free Enterprise** is seen in her original livery, featuring the 'TTF' funnel emblem of the 1975-83 period. The 1980 'Spirit Class' trio were technically identical, but could be distinguished by subtle variations in wheelhouse paintwork. *(FotoFlite)*

The **Free Enterprise VIII** is captured wearing the fresh and stylish 'TT' logo of 1984. This was to last less than four seasons. Note the 'TOWNSEND' signage positioned between her funnel and foremast which was illuminated at night time. This livery feature appeared on all but the first of the 'Free Enterprise' series. *(FotoFlite)*

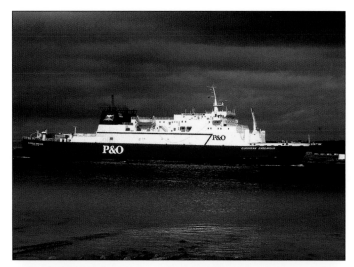

The first **European Endeavour** (formerly **European Enterprise**) is pictured with P&O's pinstripe feature along her superstructure. The former Dover based passenger vessels did not carry this aspect of the livery. *(Miles Cowsill)*

The P&O 'Euro Blue' was replaced with a deeper navy hue in the late 1990s. This helped the billowing flag emblem stand out a little more clearly on funnels such as those of the aged **Pride of Hampshire** seen here vacating Portsmouth Harbour on a morning sailing to Le Havre. *(John Hendy)*

The uncomfortable pairing of P&O and Stena Line on the Channel was aptly represented by this ungainly amalgam that appeared on funnels, in this particular case the **P&OSL Kent** (formerly the **Spirit of Free Enterprise**). *(George Holland)*

trace of Townsend Thoresen had gone, in its place a smart, if comparatively sober colour scheme of P&O 'Euro Blue' hulls and funnels. It seemed to be a visual metaphor of the transformation in culture at the Company. TT was typically bold and brash in its approach and for many years had been very successful as a result. The P&O influence appeared to be rather conservative by contrast, favouring consolidation, and latterly retreat, as opposed to expansion and innovation.

The P&O European Ferries livery was applied across their fleet fairly consistently. There were some minor anomalies though; for example the 'European' class freighters, the 'Super Vikings', and Cairnryan's *Ionic Ferry* featured a pinstripe along their superstructures which tailed off towards the bow end. The other fleet units never received this feature. The flag emblem was meant to be reversed on the starboard side of funnels so that the blue quarter always led although this was not always the case.

There was substantial heritage behind the P&O flag. Its roots were linked to the then national colours of Portugal and Spain; the countries that the vessels of the Peninsular & Oriental Steam Navigation Co. circumnavigated on their route to the Far East. Even if that obscure piece of historical fact was lost on the vast majority of passengers, the symbol remains to this day as one of service and tradition.

The creation of P&O Stena Line in 1998 saw the dominant partner's house colours favoured over Stena's cruising white scheme. In a sop to Stena, their red pinstripe was retained to sit on top of P&O's deep navy hull. However, red funnels were repainted blue and received an awkward amalgam of P&O and Stena emblems. It was clear who was in charge in this incongruent and fairly short-lived alliance.

The buyout of Stena's share in the joint company paved the way for the resurrection of the P&O Ferries brand and the adoption of a common look for the passenger fleets based at Portsmouth, Dover and Hull in 2003. This would see the blue hull colourings substantially lowered and the display of the P&O legend in much larger proportions above. The lettering continued to be inscribed in the traditional Plantin font (a serif typeface designed in the early 20th century by Frank Hinman Pierpont). The regrettable 'POferries.com' URL also made its first appearance. The sticking point with the flag emblem was always that the blue quarter lacked definition against the similarly blue funnels although thin white lines were later introduced between them. That matter was tackled when the *Spirit of Britain* emerged eight years later with non-standard white funnel casing. At the same time the URL was dropped, P&O publicists declaring that the web had reached its age of maturity and the travelling public did not need to be signposted to their site anymore.

In preparation for privatisation back in 1984, Sealink UK Ltd (formerly British Rail's Shipping & International Services Division) commissioned a total overhaul of the Sealink corporate identity. Rail Alphabet was banished, along with the 'double arrow' symbol. To represent a clean break from its railway heritage, the new Sealink livery was nothing short of revolutionary. The *Hengist* and *Horsa* were the first Channel ships to receive the new branding: funnels became navy blue, with a stylised naval epaulette symbol wrapped around in gold. Hulls became cruising white, with a striking, custom-designed new italic logotype in pale blue, complete with interlinking pinstripe. Red 'boot toppings' became navy blue. This highly innovative new livery was somewhat marred by the rather redundant addition of the 'British Ferries' tag the following year. This was an attempt by Sealink UK's new private owner, Sea Containers, to stamp their own identity on their recent acquisition. The 'British Ferries' logo would also go on to appear on the cockpits and tail end fins of Hoverspeed hovercraft in the late 1980s (another of Sea Containers' conquests).

In the dying days of the Hoverspeed operation, the British Ferries brand was but a distant memory. However, the celebration of 'Britishness' on their service was taken to the ultimate extreme when the *SeaCat Diamant* and *SeaCat Rapide* received giant Union Jack markings that spread across their hulls and superstructures. It was certainly not possible to miss them. At the time it was claimed that the livery was a tribute to England's Rugby World Cup win (the instigator of this idea clearly was not aware that the national flag of England was the Saint George's Cross, rather than the Union Flag). It was bitterly ironic that the vessels were actually built in Tasmania, registered in the Bahamas and owned by a Bermuda-based concern. The only British connection was the crews who manned them.

On the Western Channel, Brittany Ferries started out with a cruising white colour scheme that was remarkably devoid of noticeable corporate markings for a ferry company in the early 1970s. By the time that the *Cornouailles* was delivered in 1977 a nondescript orange motif was adopted on funnels, encapsulated in a wide navy blue band; a classic example of a meaningless graphic swirl being used to represent a service. With the charter of the *Goelo* in 1980, the company name was now spelt out in lower case navy lettering along hulls, sandwiched in between the aforementioned motif either side and corresponding navy and orange wraparound pinstripes. This was not to be the last time that a cluster of coloured lines would be utilised.

The Rook Dunning design agency created an updated look for Brittany Ferries in 1984: the lower case sans serif characters were replaced with a more dignified slab serif typeface while the graphic swirl was simplified into a flag/wave emblem. It was a case of gradualism rather than revolution. When the *Bretagne* arrived in 1989 she deviated from the established fleet livery scheme through the introduction of multiple navy stripes around her superstructure and a pronounced kink in her navy/orange pinstripe at the stern end. She looked flashy and trendy for her time. And even a quarter of a century later she still somehow gives the impression of being ahead of her time: A brilliantly designed ferry indeed.

There was a further modification to the Brittany Ferries corporate identity in 2002 but its actual implementation on vessels was an extraordinarily protracted matter. Ironically, the *Mont St Michel* was delivered late that year with the old 1984-style lettering and funnel markings, instead of the new italic moniker and elongated flag/wave logo:

The first vessel in the fleet to wear the new look was the *Pont-Aven* of 2004. The last vessel to conform was the *Barfleur* as late as 2009. However, there were many jarring inconsistencies in the

When P&O and Stena pooled their services on the Eastern Channel, the resulting livery was an interesting hybrid of their liveries. The Garamond font was used to display the joint trading name along hulls and superstructures. The **European Seaway** is seen here in the Dover Straits being passed by the **Stena Empereur/P&OSL Provence**. *(FotoFlite)*

The **Stena Cambria** is seen here approaching Calais in the 1996 revision of the Stena Line livery. This was implemented across all sectors of the Company's operations, bringing to an end 24 years of the Sealink brand in the United Kingdom. Note the shield motif on her prow and the trading name off-set to the forward end of her hull. *(Miles Cowsill)*

The **SeaCat Rapide** is seen here tied up along The Prince of Wales Pier at Dover on the very last day of Hoverspeed operations in early November 2005. The livery could, at best, be described as eye-catching. On such an unconventional looking passenger vessel, it probably wasn't so out of place. *(George Holland)*

The **Quiberon** is seen during 1982, her first year of Brittany Ferries service. She made her debut on the Plymouth/Santander route wearing the 1980 revision of the Company's livery which included the display of the trading name for the first time. *(Ferry Publications Library)*

The **Bretagne** is seen leaving Portsmouth Harbour during the Summer of 2006, looking very much as she did when delivered in 1989, the only differences being the raising of her navy blue 'boot topping' (to help conceal the rust-prone lower works) and the unfortunate 'stability blister' added as the result of more stringent safety regulations. *(George Holland)*

It wasn't until six years after her debut, that the **Mont St Michel** adopted the current Brittany Ferries livery. However it was applied inaccurately, with inconsistencies in styles and proportions. *(George Holland)*

appearance of the Brittany Ferries fleet: the *Armorique* and *Barfleur* were devoid of the navy/orange bands around their funnels. The lettering was out of proportion and applied without stencils on the *Bretagne, Mont St Michel* and the *Normandie,* resulting in remarkably clumsy depictions of the logo. This was rather surprising considering a company of Brittany Ferries' stature. Consistency and coherence are often associated with quality and professionalism. How odd that a company renowned for the attention to detail of its on-board services can fail to get its exterior markings right on some of its vessels.

When Transmanche Ferries was set up in 2001, its livery was effectively dictated by the colour scheme inherited on the chartered *Sardinia Vera.* The Sardinia Ferries livery of yellow hull and deep navy funnel was retained and simply added to with a vulgar turquoise 'T' in a roundel: Crude, but effective. When the *Côte d'Albâtre* and *Seven Sisters* were delivered in 2006 they adopted wholly yellow funnels and embraced that most unfortunate marketing device of the decade; the giant URL: 'WWW.TRANSMANCHEFERRIES.COM' was emblazoned along their hulls and stubbornly remains to this day, despite URLs falling out of fashion with other operators.

The floating URL concept reached its zenith in 2008 when the 'norfolkline.com' legend was painted in enormous proportions along the superstructures of the Norfolkline Dover/Dunkirk ships. The result was drastic to say the least. They had taken three smart modern vessels, with nice touches of styling, and effectively desecrated them. The lettering was not even in their corporate font!

All change occurred in 2011 when the DFDS Seaways brand was introduced on the Channel in the wake of Norfolkline's acquisition by fellow Danish shipping giant, DFDS. They appear to have embraced P&O's previous colour scheme, with navy blue funnels and hulls. The Maltese cross emblem is rooted in the history of the Company and certainly looks clean cut and respectable within a roundel. This comparitively conservative livery is, arguably, rather flattering on their vessels, and suggests that DFDS Seaways wishes to be seen as a serious player on the Channel, rather than a cheap and nasty upstart.

The continued expansion of DFDS Seaways into the Channel ferry market saw the phasing out of LD Lines as a separate brand in this sector. Established in 2005 to fill the gap left by P&O's abandoned Portsmouth/Le Havre service, LD Lines was a small outfit with big ambitions, but questionable strategies. They seemed intent on Channel domination and by 2010 they had involvement in four routes. However, their retreat was as sudden as their previous proliferation. Virtually the only steady factor during their first eight years of existence was the presence in their fleet of their pioneering vessel, *Norman Spirit* (although she was operated as *Ostend Spirit* in conjunction with the now defunct TransEuropa Ferries for one of those years). This ferry has had a literally colourful history; wearing the liveries of seven different operators (Oostende/Dover Line, Oostende Lines, P&O Stena Line, P&O Ferries, LD Lines, LD Lines/TransEuropa Ferries and currently DFDS Seaways) and in that time she has sailed under a total of seven different names to date (*Prins Filip, Stena Royal, P&OSL Aquitaine, Pride of Aquitaine, Norman Spirit,*

P&O's *European Endeavour* (II) is seen here in detail during her brief spell on the Dover/Calais route. In a previous incarnation she was known to Channel travellers as Norfolkline's *Midnight Merchant*. She is currently employed on the Irish Sea. It would seem that the ro-pax type vessels in the P&O fleet have retained full height blue hulls. *(John Hendy)*

When the **Barfleur** was overhauled at Dunkirk in early 2013 she belatedly received an accurate application of the Brittany Ferries trademarks. However, her funnels were still inexplicably devoid of the standard wraparound stripes. *(George Holland)*

The faithful **Norman Spirit** is seen in her final LD Lines incarnation. The roller coaster style hull paintwork is further accentuated by a wavering red stripe above. In all, it seemed to visually sum up the rather volatile nature of the Company's operations on the Channel: Up one month and down the next. *(George Holland)*

An unusual sight at Dover: The Transmanche Ferries branded **Côte d'Albâtre** had a short-lived spell on LD Lines' abortive Dover/Boulogne service during 2009. She is now back on the Newhaven/Dieppe route, under the banner of DFDS Seaways, but the vivid yellow livery persists at the insistence of the vessel's owner, the Conseil General de Seine Maritime. *(George Holland)*

The former **Norman Spirit** looks much more shipshape as the **Calais Seaways**. Here it can be been seen that DFDS's iconic Maltese cross symbol has been welded to the funnel lattice work quite effectively. *(George Holland)*

Clean lines and a flattering livery give DFDS Seaways' Dover/Dunkirk vessels a dignified and pleasing new look. The similarity to the P&O European Ferries colour scheme of the late 1980s is interesting. Here **Dunkerque Seaways** is pictured arriving at Dunkirk West during the Summer of 2011. *(George Holland)*

The **Berlioz** is seen here unusually devoid of her port side lifeboats. It can be seen, apart from the regrettable change of brand name, that the essence of the SeaFrance livery lives on with virtually the same colour scheme in use. *(George Holland)*

Ostend Spirit, Norman Spirit, Calais Seaways). During her tenure with LD Lines her livery was modified three times, culminating in what must go down in industry history as one of the most spectacularly hideous paint schemes she has ever suffered the indignity of wearing.

And the latest brand to grace the waves is 'MyFerryLink'. If it is possible to forgive the terribly naff name, MFL (the acronym sounds more credible for a ferry operator than the unfortunate unabbreviated version) has a remarkably similar colour scheme to its previous incarnation (SeaFrance). Indeed, virtually the whole SeaFrance operation has been inherited lock, stock and barrel, by MFL, to include the same house colours. But whereas SeaFrance used an elegant typeface to display its trademark (along with a stylised expression of the French tricolour shaped into the company's 'S' initial), MyFerryLink has opted for vulgar, broad lettering accompanied by a meaningless graphic swirl. Meaningless graphic swirls? Now there's an unoriginal idea!

In warmer climes it is possible to find some of the most outlandish ferry liveries in the world. One operator, Italy's Moby Lines, stands out as the pioneer of truly wacky paint schemes. Over the years their trademark lettering has got bigger – to the extent it now stretches from waterline to boat decks on many of their ferries. Their unmistakable whale motif (inspired by the legendary 'Moby Dick') has conversely become upstaged on many of their fleet members by a veritable array of Warner Brothers' 'Looney Tunes' characters. These have been reproduced in gigantic proportions under licence from their American creators. Moby Lines have some potentially very attractive modern ships in their fleet. However, their elegant lines are utterly bombarded by the madcap cartoon creations. Each vessel has its own unique variation on the 'Looney Tunes' theme. The results are certainly fun and remarkably different to anything else in the industry. And perhaps that is precisely what Moby have sought to achieve: A livery that is outrageous and varies wildly from one vessel to another, yet is instantly identifiable as Moby. An interesting paradox indeed, considering the earlier discussion of the virtues of consistency and coherence.

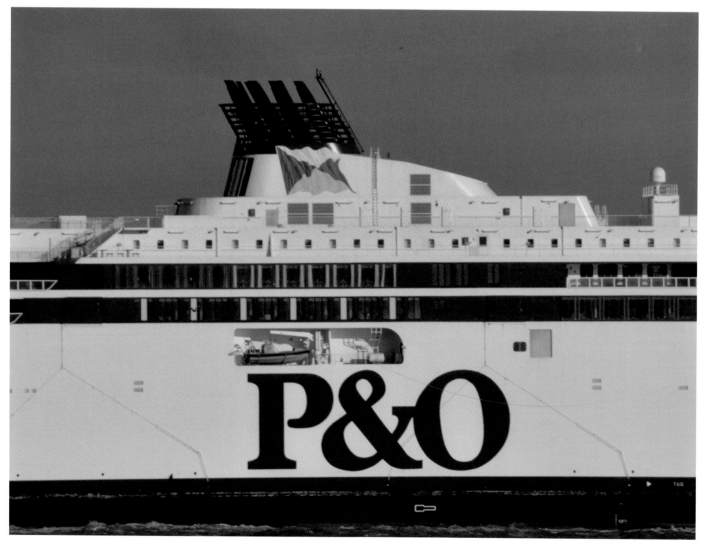

White funnels appear to be a unique feature of Dover's 'Spirit 2'. Their fleet mates have yet to come into line. The elaborate artwork of the billowing flag emblem has been painted on directly using stencils. The 'P&O' lettering is displayed in gigantic proportions using the elegant Plantin font. It is particularly distinctive by dint of the condensed kerning (the spacing between each letter). *(George Holland)*

12 Bridging the Gulf: Tallinn-Helsinki
by Matthew Punter

THE PEACE DIVIDEND

The collapse of the Iron Curtain in 1989 and the dissolution of the USSR two years later have transformed the whole of Europe. Former foes are now firm friends and trade and travel have increased exponentially. A visit to Vilnius or Bratislava, once viewed as exotic, bordering on the preposterous, is now as commonplace as Edinburgh or Paris.

The expansion of European commerce in the intervening decades has seen a flowering of shipping routes as companies have moved to serve the growing demand. The Baltic has been the major beneficiary with three main spheres having seen dramatic growth since the curtain fell. Firstly, there have been the long-haul freight or ro-pax services linking the German Baltic coast, bypassing Poland and terminating in one of the Baltic states or Russia. Secondly, there has been the expansion of the trans-Baltic cruise ferry services from Stockholm which has targeted new territory in Estonia and Latvia. Thirdly, and most remarkably, has been the rapid rise of the short-sea route between Helsinki and Tallinn. Prior to 1989 the service was a backwater, a footnote to any overview of European passenger shipping. By 2013, it had become one of the most impressive shipping routes on the continent with four long-term, committed operators servicing the connection with a largely newly built fleet and offering passengers a variety of products to suit all-comers from the party-goer through to the bargain-hunter.

Northern Europe's high-intensity short-sea routes are amongst the continent's most fascinating. Whilst the overnight crossings attract the greatest renown, with their elegant, liner-like vessels and distant echoes of a lost age of panama-hatted, ocean-going romance, it is the workaday services, sailing from the busiest ports that generate not only the most traffic, but also the most interest. Frequent crossings, regular fleet renewal and the sheer logistical complexities of such services demonstrate the ferryman's craft at its most brilliant. Each day, at Dover, Frederikshavn, Puttgarden, Helsingborg and Tallinn, hundreds of departures bring tens of thousands of passengers and their vehicles to their chosen destination in comfort, safety and style. This is the story of the latest jewel in this maritime crown.

SAILING THROUGH THE CURTAIN

The origins of the modern Tallinn-Helsinki service date from 1965. In that year, the Estonian Shipping Company (ESCO) commenced a peak season passenger service between the two ports, utilising the motor vessel *Vanemuine*. The service was the passenger sea route to link the USSR with 'free' Europe and most of the traffic consisted of Finns travelling to see their mysterious neighbours, so close, yet so immensely far away. The inaugural vessel was replaced for the 1967 season with a similar, but larger ship, the *Svanetiya* which was renamed the *Tallinn* for her new

The first ferry to serve Tallinn – Helksinki was the **Vanemuine**. *(Histrodamus)*

role. At the same time, the route became a year-round operation. In 1980, the route moved into the car-ferry era with the arrival of the newly built *Georg Ots*. She was the lead vessel in an extensive series of modern, yet smallish, car ferries: a sort of Soviet Papenburg class that spread far and wide from the Szczecin shipyard in north-western Poland from which they originated, reaching Istanbul, Odessa, Leningrad, Vladivostok and many points in between.

The *Georg Ots* continued a very Soviet style of service for the remainder of the decade, the only interlude being a brief spell at Reykjavik during the Reagan-Gorbachev summit in October 1986. On board her main deck, Gorbachev and his advisors discussed their approach to strategic arms reduction. It was a role that perhaps augured well for the future of her line as a little over three years later, in one momentous night, the cracks became a cavity, the cavity a chasm and the wall came crumbling down. The Iron Curtain was no more.

Such was the spirit of freedom sweeping across the Soviet Bloc that steps had already been taken to modernise the ferry link several months before. In May 1989, ESCO and the Finnish operator Palkkiyhtymä Oy, together with the City and Port of Tallinn, had established a subsidiary called Tallink to commence a new operation on the route. The company purchased the former Silja ferry *Svea Regina*, latterly with SeaEscape in the Bahamas, and introduced her as the *Tallink* in January 1990. She was joined later in the season by the freighter *Trans Estonia*.

In March 1991, a referendum in Estonia set the Soviet satellite on the road to independence which was duly declared on 20th August that year, heralding not just a new hope for this forgotten corner of the world, but a new dawn for relations between the Scandinavian and Baltic lands either side of the sea.

It wasn't just ESCO and their new partners who were making hay whilst the Baltic sun shone: several other operators were by now actively pursuing their own plans for commencing trade between the two ports. The Estonian company Inreko established Festa Line in 1991, with Aeroflot taking 20 per cent of the business, which operated passenger only hydrofoils between Tallinn and Helsinki. The Åland-based Eckerö Linjen had also been evaluating the potential for several years but in the end, decided to charter a vessel to Inreko. Operating under the brand name Estonian New Line, Brittany Ferries' *Corbière* duly commenced service late in 1991 trading throughout the following year. The Festa Line hydrofoils were also operated under this new brand from the same time. For winter 1992-3, Eckerö became more involved, adding their *Roslagen* (one of the many Papenburg-built sisters of the *Corbière*) as Estonian New Line became a joint operation.

Whilst the Estonian New Line business developed, ESCO and Tallink were consolidating, with the former withdrawing from the route as their own entity in late 1991 and chartering the *Georg Ots* to their subsidiary, thus focusing their energies on competing with the newcomers rather than within their own group. Further consolidation occurred in early 1993 when Inreko ended their partnership with Eckerö and instead joined ESCO in the Tallink operation, the joint Inreko/ESCO parent company being named AS Eminre. The Estonian New Line brand was dropped and the 'new' Tallink utilised the *Tallink*, the *Georg Ots*, the *Corbière*, the *Trans Estonia* and the hydrofoils. Irish Ferries' *Saint Patrick II* also started over-wintering regularly to provide additional capacity from 1992.

Eckerö did not give up, however, and in August 1994, they partnered with Birka Line to launch the first wholly Finnish service on the route. The new operation was named Eestin-Linjat ('Estonian Line') and was launched with the *Alandia*, another Papenburg-built ferry. Inreko meanwhile, had purchased the *Thor Heyerdahl* from Nordström & Thulin and she became the lead Tallink vessel from May 1994, carrying the name *Vana Tallinn* (Old Tallinn). That same year, Eminre split into two operations with the Helsinki operation transferring to A/S Hansatee, retaining the Tallink brand. The other part of the company was responsible for a short-lived service to Travemünde.

The apparent riches to be gained from the Helsinki-Tallinn route were becoming increasingly attractive to the more longstanding shipping companies on the Baltic Sea. Viking Line made their first, tentative, step into the waters during summer 1994 with the charter of the passenger-only *Condor 9*, marketed as 'Viking Express', although due to union issues, this service was not a success. Another approach was being taken by Silja who used the *Silja Festival* on an experimental 24-hour cruise circuit from Helsinki to Tallinn from September 1994. The company's *Wasa Queen* was also utilized over the same period.

Scarcely had the dust settled on the febrile 1994 summer season when disaster struck, with the sinking of Estline's *Estonia* during a major storm, whilst on passage from Tallinn to Stockholm on the night of 27th September 1994, resulting in the loss of 852 lives. That such a calamity could befall a large and modern ferry had huge and immediate ramifications for the industry. Passengers took fright and most services saw a dramatic reduction in traffic which took several years to recover.

Inreko's Estonian New Line service commenced with the **Corbiere** in 1992. *(Jukka Huotari)*

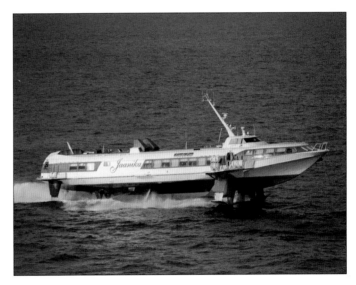

Linda Line's **Jaanika** approaches Helsinki. *(Jukka Huotari)*

Silja's **Finnjet** loads at Helsinki's Katajanokka ferry terminal for another crossing to Tallinn. *(Matthew Punter)*

CONSOLIDATION

Despite the Hansatee re-organisation, Inreko and ESCO parted ways after less than two years in early 1995 with the *Vana Tallinn* thenceforth chartered to Tallink. Even this state of affairs was short-lived with a total breakdown in relations occurring in late 1996 when Inreko cancelled the charter and established their own rival service as TH Ferries in December of that year. At the same time, they also withdrew the hydrofoils from the service, and Linda Line was established using the *Liisa*, the *Laura* and the *Jaanika*.

Tallink replaced the *Vana Tallinn* with a charter of the *Mare Balticum* (the *Estonia*'s replacement for Estline). She made her debut as the *Meloodia* in September 1996. To make doubly sure that their former comrades would not gain the upper hand, early in 1997 the *Stena Normandy* arrived on a one-year charter with the *Tallink* being withdrawn. They also acquired the *Sleipner*, a replacement fast ferry in lieu of the lost hydrofoils, which was renamed *Tallink Express 1*.

However, as a result of the rapid expansion and cut-throat competition during this period, Tallink ended up in severe financial difficulties. In 1997, the company was taken over by two Estonian businessmen, Enn Pant and Ain Hanschmidt, both with connections to the country's finance industry. Together, they took close and immediate control of the business with ambitious plans for future success.

Immediately, dividends were reaped for the new owners as Tallink's recent expansion meant that TH Ferries failed to gain traction. In January 1998, the operation folded and the *Vana Tallinn* was sold back to Tallink. They simultaneously also acquired the *Lion King* to operate as the *Fantaasia* whilst the *Normandy* returned to her owners. The 1998 line-up featured the *Meloodia*, *Fantaasia*, *Vana Tallinn* and the *Georg Ots* with the *Tallink Express* on fast passenger duties.

Whilst the Tallink soap opera was being resolved, the other operators on the route continued to experiment and develop. Viking Line returned to the route for 1995 with a car-carrying catamaran, the *Condor 10*, and then over the 1995-6 winter season introduced the *Cinderella* on 24-hour cruises. This was a huge vote of confidence in the growing short-cruise market as the *Cinderella* was Viking's largest and most luxurious cruise ferry. The *Silja Festival* also returned for a second winter on these increasingly popular trips which typically left Helsinki in the late evening, cruised slowly overnight to Tallinn where there was time ashore to stock up on (prodigious) quantities of alcohol and other products, before a leisurely amble back across the Gulf of Finland in the late afternoon. In 1997, the mighty *Finnjet* took over Silja's service although the destination became Muuga, a short distance east of Tallinn. She maintained this service year-round although during the summer operated Helsinki-Tallinn-Travemünde. From 1999, her Estonian terminal became Tallinn proper.

Eestin-Linjat had also grown and in 1998 introduced significantly more modern tonnage with the arrival of the *Nordlandia*, formerly Nordström & Thulin's *Nord Gotlandia*, in February 1998. She adopted a different pattern again, essentially offering daytime cruises from Helsinki with a morning departure and overnight return, with frequency increasing during the peak season. Eckerö adopted their own name for the route from this time. By this stage, both Tallink and Eckerö were operating from the West Harbour in Helsinki which had opened in 1995, leaving Silja and (intermittently) Viking to sail from the traditional South Harbour. This gave both operators room to expand although meant that passengers could no longer walk from the terminals into the city centre.

In less than ten years since the arrival of a modern ferry service on the route, there was now an impressive smörgåsbord of different options: conventional day ferries, overnight cruises, fast car ferries and passenger hydrofoils. The future would see Helsinki-Tallinn moving centre stage: powered by Pant and Hanschmidt, it was to become the engine that drove the growth of the entire sector over the next decade.

THE FAST FERRY ERA

The next phase of development focused on high-speed services as several operators added numerous craft of various designs. The route was in many ways an obvious opportunity for fast ferries. It linked two attractive and thriving capital cities; the waters were seldom disturbed by bad weather, although were ice-bound between December and Easter; the existing ferries were arguably a means to an end (the end being cheap booze) and the day-cruise fleet was somewhat lacking in the thrusting modernity associated with the zeitgeist of the coming millennium.

Helta Line were first to the scene with their hydrofoils *Sinilind* and *Luik* in 1990. The Inreko/Aeroflot-backed Festa Line started operation with the *Tsiklon* in 1991 and quickly bought out Helta. The fleet was then absorbed into Estonian New Line, then Tallink, with the baton finally passing to Linda Line from 1997. Viking Line were also early movers, but struggled and after a final attempt in 1996 with two passenger-only catamarans, turned their attention to the cruise service where their expertise lay.

Somewhat unexpectedly, it was the German company FRS who established the first really successful fast car-ferry service between the two ports in 1998. FRS originated as a shopping excursion operator across the Flensburg fjord between Germany and Denmark, which had grown to include services to Helgoland, the Sylt-Rømø car ferry connection and services on the Baltic coast of the former East Germany. Trading as Nordic Jet Line, they arrived purposefully, with Norwegian Kværner-built catamarans, somewhat smaller than the more typical InCat or Austal designs of the time. The *Nordic Jet* opened the route in June 1998 with her sister *Baltic Jet* arriving the following year. They operated from the South Harbour in Helsinki, taking a terminal north of the Viking Line berth and therefore within very easy walk of the city centre.

One can only imagine the consternation in Tallink Towers. Pant and Hanschmidt were still arranging the stationery on their desks yet here was a German upstart – throwing aluminium spanners in their carefully financed works. Predictably, they were quick to respond.

In 1999, Tallink introduced their first car-carrying catamaran, the *Tallink AutoExpress*, which was a very early Austal design, previously operating for DSB and Cat-Link. She was joined in 2001 by half-sister *Boomerang* from Polferries, renamed the *Tallink AutoExpress 2*.

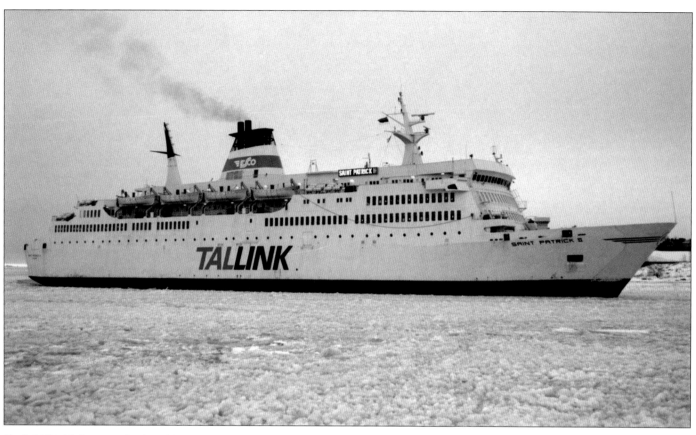

The **Saint Patrick II** was a regular winter visitor to Tallink during the early 1990s. *(Jukka Huotari)*

Showing the Inreko logo on her funnel, the **Vana Tallinn** is seen turning in Helsinki's South Harbour. *(Jukka Huotari)*

The **Corbiere** returned to the route as the **Apollo** for Eestin-Linjat during the mid 1990s. *(Jukka Huotari)*

ESCO's **Georg Ots** became the first car ferry on the link from 1980, seen here in Tallink/ESCO colours in 1995. *(Jukka Huotari)*

Whilst all this was occurring, there were also big changes on the opposite side of the Gulf of Finland with Sea Containers taking control of Silja Line. The arrival of Sea Containers saw an immediate focus on fast ferry services with the company introducing their *SuperSeaCat Four* onto the Helsinki-Tallinn route in 2000, adding a fast day option to the *Finnjet* cruise service. The *SuperSeaCat Four* was a Fincantieri-built monohull, offering a sleeker profile but no more enjoyable experience than the twin-hull craft at the time favoured by FRS and Tallink.

Still, there was a war on and the fast ferry arms race continued unabated. Silja introduced a second vessel, the *SuperSeaCat Three* in 2003 and Tallink responded the following year with a further two craft, the *Tallink AutoExpress 3* and the *Tallink AutoExpress 4*, both of which were earlier derivations of Silja's sisters, having been built speculatively as the *Pegasus Two* and *Pegasus One* in the mid-1990s.

Of course, the rapid growth in the fast ferry services had a significant impact on Linda Line. Having had the fast market to themselves for most of the 1990s, the ferocious competition from FRS, Tallink and Silja proved a significant challenge. The company introduced a new Russian-built passenger catamaran, the *Linda Express*, in 2002 but her first season was beset by mishaps and although she soldiered on through 2003 she was soon sold and the company continued with its hydrofoils. Eventually, in 2007 a new catamaran, the *Merilin*, was purchased and she was joined by the *Karolin* in 2008.

A NEW GENERATION

Pant and Hanschmidt were in it for the long game however; the fast ferry skirmish being something of a sideshow to their principle desire to see Tallink emerge as equal, if not superior, to their rivals. It was insufficient to be dominant in the day-cruise and fast ferry market, a solution was needed for the overnight traffic also. In August 2000, the company placed an order with Åker Finnyards for a 41,000 gross tonnes cruise ferry. Although she was not the largest vessel constructed for the region, she was certainly the first for over a decade and a welcome return to form for the Baltic ferry industry, even if the Estonians were now making the running rather than the Swedes or Finns. She would offer the full spectrum of Baltic cruise ferry facilities, including a two-deck show lounge and a spa area.

The new *Romantika* arrived in May 2002, replacing the *Fantaasia* which moved to the Tallinn-Stockholm route, under Tallink control since 2001. Although lacking the dramatic and lavish interiors of the previous generation of vessels, the *Romantika* set the standard for a fresh decade of ferry investment and it was clear that the centre of gravity now lay in the east. An early illustration of the changing fortunes came in 2003 when Viking Line, unable to compete with the shiny new ship (and her cheaper crew), withdrew their *Cinderella* from the cruise circuit. She was replaced with the *Rosella* on a day-cruise schedule.

The year 2006 was truly paradigm shifting for the industry as Tallink purchased firstly the Hanko-Rostock operation and ships of Superfast and then later in the year achieved their *coup de grâce* with the takeover of Silja Line. Although they were prohibited from operating the SuperSeaCats, which were spun off into an

A busy scene at Tallinn with the **Meloodia**, **Fantaasia** and **Vana Tallinn** all awaiting sailings to Helsinki during July 2000. *(Matthew Punter)*

The unsuccessful **Linda Express** during her brief spell with Linda Line. *(Jukka Huotari)*

Eckerö Line's **Nordlandia** arrived in 1998 to re-invigorate her owner's presence on the route. *(Matthew Punter)*

Viking Line chartered the **Condor 10** as their first car ferry on the service in 1995. *(Jukka Huotari)*

The **Meloodia** joined the service in 1996 having previously operated for Estline as their **Mare Balticum**. *(Jukka Huotari)*

independent operation, essentially, their dominance was complete. It was not only a corporate shopping spree that Tallink had indulged in; since the arrival of the *Romantika* in 2002, they had also been ordering a sequence of increasingly impressive cruise ferries. The *Victoria I*, a sister to the *Romantika*, arrived in 2004 for the Tallinn-Stockholm route and an enlarged version of the class, the *Galaxy*, went onto the Tallinn-Helsinki route in 2006. She in turn was replaced by a younger sister, the *Baltic Princess*, in 2008 and the *Baltic Queen* joined the Swedish route in 2009.

With the cruise circuit in safe hands, a solution was also sought for the fast ferry and day cruise operations. Tallink turned once again to Åker, ordering a large and, crucially, fast day ferry which arrived in 2007 as the *Star*. A second order was placed with Fincantieri for the *Superstar*, based on a successful Moby Lines design that would partner the *Star* from 2008. Both ships offered superb facilities with buffets, business class, huge shopping facilities and various bars, cafés and lounges.

The arrival of these ships, complete with lurid, lime green liveries, saw the day cruise operation repositioned as the 'Tallink Shuttle', offering up to six departures a day with overnight crossings being handled by the *Baltic Princess*. The short-sea old guard was redundant: *Vana Tallinn*, *Meloodia*, *Fantaasia* and the 'Tallink AutoExpresses' were all disposed of. The other fast ferries were doomed also: both Nordic Jet Line and SuperSeaCat soldiered on into 2008 with one craft each before finally calling it quits at the end of that season. Only Linda Line continue with their summer- and passenger-only service.

Viking Line's response was interesting and innovative; having tried both overnight and day cruise operations, in 2008 they introduced the purpose-built *Viking XPRS*, a hybrid ship that could serve both markets with fast daytime crossings and a leisurely night-time leg where Finns (and returning Estonians) could let their hair down in traditional style.

Finally, late to the party as ever, Eckerö Line returned fire with the purchase of the *Moby Freedom* (the *Superstar*'s older sister), refurbished for Baltic service as the *Finlandia*, entering service on New Year's Eve 2012. Resolutely Finnish, she maintained her owner's proclivity for morning departures from Helsinki carrying hordes of compatriots on what is a very well-constructed product that knows its target market perfectly.

TO THE FUTURE

The remarkable story of Tallinn-Helsinki is of course borne out through a set of unique circumstances; geographical, economic, political but perhaps most importantly through the vision and leadership of the key players. Recent developments have seen not only the arrival of the *Finlandia*, but also the *Silja Europa* on the Tallink cruise operation. With the introduction of the impressive – and competing – *Viking Grace* at Turku, the *Baltic Princess* was required to shore up Tallink's position on this route. The *Silja Europa* is in any case better suited to the rigours of the shorter crossing with her worn interior being less obvious when one is face down on the carpet – which Tallinn-Helsinki cruise passengers are wont to be. Apparently.

A visit to the area in early 2013 demonstrated four very distinct products: the *Finlandia* for a great Finnish day out; Tallink Shuttle

Silja's **Superseacat Three** speeds away from Tallinn en route to Helsinki during her spell on the service. *(Matthew Punter)*

Tallink's original fast car ferry **Tallink AutoExpress** approaches Tallinn in September 2005. *(Matthew Punter)*

Tallink port at its busiest with (left to right) the **Romantika**, **Victoria 1**, **Nordlandia** and Tallink **AutoExpress3**. *(Matthew Punter)*

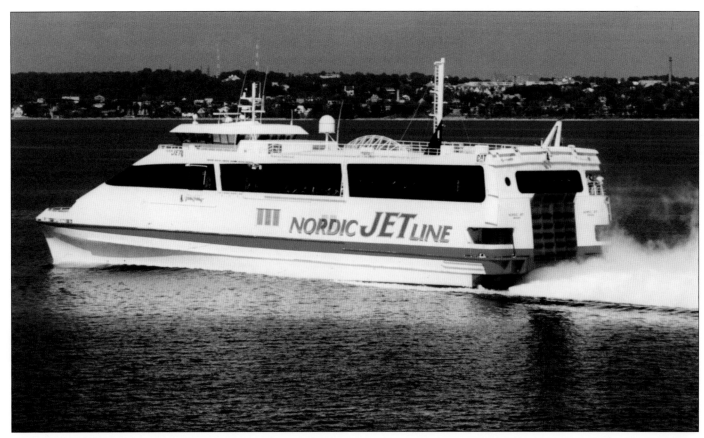

Nordic Jet Line's **Nordic Jet** is seen speeding away from Tallinn in July 2000. *(Matthew Punter)*

The **Merilin** joined the Linda Line service in 2006. *(Kalle Id)*

Tallink chartered the **Normandy** for the 1997 season to see off the threat of TH Ferries. *(Jukka Huotari)*

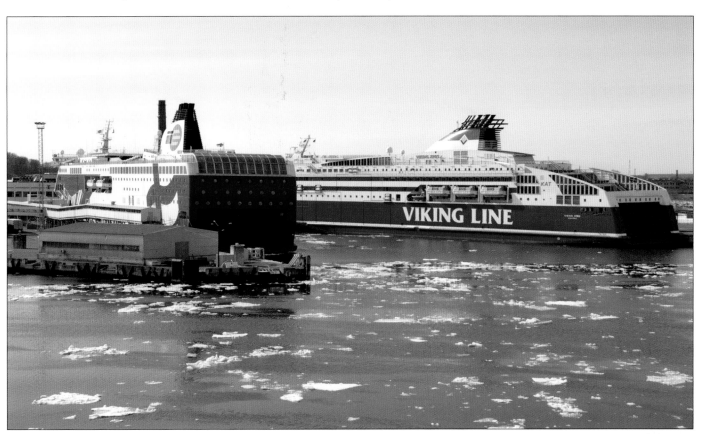

The **Finlandia** and **Viking XPRS** load at Tallinn in April 2013. *(Matthew Punter)*

An early morning scene at Tallinn as the **Silja Europa** loads. *(Matthew Punter)*

The **Viking XPRS** at Tallinn during April 2013. *(Matthew Punter)*

for the more upmarket shopper and traveller; the *Silja Europa* for the rambunctious party crowd and the *Viking Grace* for everyone else. And perhaps that points to the next phase of the route's development. Faced with rising costs, in 2014 Viking Line will transfer the *Viking XPRS* to the Estonian flag; but where does that really leave the operation, having neither the frequency of departures to attract regular traffic nor the calibre of ship to attract the party crowd?

The history of the service has been fascinating, acting as a microcosm for a wide variety of different industry models. Although none of the operators are likely to be investing in the near future, a degree of consolidation is foreseeable. It is certain however, that the route will remain one of the most varied and interesting in the whole of Europe.

Tallink's first newbuilding was the **Romantika** which introduced their first proper cruise concept in 2002. *(Matthew Punter)*

12 Alaska Marine Highway System
by William Barham

As the cruise brochures show, Alaska offers grand scenery, forests, mountains, glaciers, blue skies, ice flows and rich marine wildlife. During its brief summer, Alaska can be stunning. What the brochures don't reveal are the huge challenges to marine navigation not only from its treacherous coast, but rough waters, tidal ranges, fog, depressions, perishing temperatures, high winds, ice and snow. Few coastal communities have road connections and if one adds to this this factors such as high seasonal variations in passenger numbers, a largely worn out fleet, financial constraints from being a public service operator, as well as air and sea-freight completion then it clear that Alaska's Marine Highway System (AMHS) has exceptionally challenging conditions.

AMHS traces its heritage back to 1949 when local entrepreneurs set up landing craft service from Juneau with a single war surplus LCT. The mv *Chilkoot* as she was re-named had capacity for 13 cars and 20 passengers. Although the operation was taken over by Alaskan Territorial Road Commissioners in 1951 and purpose built *Chalikat* took over in 1957 with capacity for 15 vehicles and 59 passengers, initial development was slow. This changed in 1959 when Alaska was granted 'statehood' and coastal connections with the 'lower 48' needed to be improved.

The vision of a linear ferry network somewhat similar to Norway's Hurtigruten emerged and bonds were issued by the new state enabling the construction of a new fleet designed by the notable Seattle marine architect Philip Spaulding drawing on experience from Black Ball's *Coho* (1959) and BC Ferries' *Sidney* (1960). Initially, four vessels were constructed:

Three 352ft 'mainliners'- the *Malaspina* (1962), *Taku* (1962) and *Matanuska* (1963) each with capacity for 500 passengers, 100 berths and 109 vehicles to connect south-eastern communities with the road networks in northern BC and Washington.

The 240ft *Tustumena* (1964) to link communities along the Kodiak and Kenai peninsula in south west Alaska.

Since their inauguration 50 years ago, all except the *Taku* have been rebuilt and extended as demand has grown. Other units have been added as the network expanded and today's fleet numbers nine conventional vessels and two fast-craft..

A significant early development was the purchase of the *Stena Britannica* (1967) in 1968. She was re-named *Wickersham* to improve the Prince Rupert and Seattle links. Although offering impressive facilities, she was not commercially successful as her bow door- stern door loading arrangements limited the number of ports she could serve and her draft required her to make longer open sea passages to Sitka, the historic Russian settlement on Baranof Island. The *Wickersham's* usefulness was further constrained by the Jones Act with which she could not comply and in 1974 she was sold on to Rederi Ab Sally as the *Viking 6*.

AMHS ordered a replacement flagship from Lockheed shipbuilding in 1972 who delivered the fleet's largest vessel: 418ft *Colombia* (1974) with capacity for 1,000 passengers, 312 berths and 158 vehicles standard. Although retaining Spaulding's aerodynamic lines, she also incorporated many pleasing passenger features from the *Wickersham* including a full service restaurant.

Smaller 'Spaulding' designed units to provide connection services have been added: the smallest in the fleet - 193ft *Bartlett* (1969) with capacity for 190 passengers and 41 vehicles which was replaced by a fast-craft in 2005 and the 235ft sisters *Le Conte* (1974) and *Aurora* (1977) with capacity for 250 passengers and 44 vehicles.

More recently the 380ft *Kennicott* was delivered in 1998 with capacity for 434 passengers 314 berths and over 100 vehicles. Funded out of compensation paid to State of Alaska following the *Exxon Valdez* oil spill and environmental catastrophe, she has a secondary mission to respond to pollution incidents for which she carries specialist equipment and equipped with a flight deck.

Most recent additions to the fleet have been two fast-craft, which AMHS had designed to their own specifications and have caused on-going controversy about suitability and durability. Smallest in the fleet, *Lituya* (2004) with capacity for 149 passengers and 18 vehicles serves communities close to Ketchikan.

Today, AMHS's operates in three areas:

1.　South-eastern service which runs from Bellingham for Seattle, or Prince Rupert, BC to Ketchikan, Juneau, Skagway and all points in between on which the *Taku, Matasuska, Columbia* and *Kennicott* are deployed. During the last few summers, capacity has been supplemented by the *Malaspina* operating round trip sailings along the Lynn Channel from Juneau to Skagway each day.

This core route is supported by feeder services to island communities using the smaller 'day-boats'. Separately funded by local communities, Alaska's Inter-Island Ferry Authority service link Ketchikan with Hollis on Prince of Wales Island using at any one time, just one of their powerful, purpose built twins *Skina* and *Prince of Wales*.

2.　Cross Gulf services providing road links from Valdez and Cordova to Whittier for Anchorage using the *Aurora* and fast-craft.

3.　Aleutian Island chain service from Homer on the mainland to Dutch Harbour 600 miles west in the Pacific Ocean with eleven calling points. This is a 9 day roundtrip journey offered fortnightly on the old 'Trusty' *Tustumena* (1964), one of the Spaulding originals.

Across these areas, different vehicle loading procedures are in use which limits fleet utilisation and interchangeability. For example the main south-eastern services utilise a stern and forward side-door arrangement requiring vehicles to turn 90

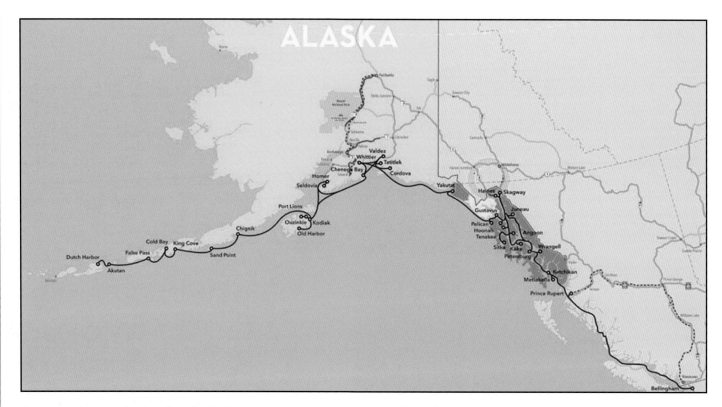

degrees on board to load or disembark. This arrangement accounts for the vessels' wide-beams and often means that loading and unloading is a lengthy process, requiring much marshalling on the car deck as the vessels make multiple stops.

Local services on the *Aurora*, *Le Conte* and fast-craft use simple stern and bow door arrangements whilst the Aleutian services requires vehicle hoists as vessels simply tie up against docks lacking any kind of linkspan. Uniquely, the *Kennicott* was designed with vehicle hoists as well as side and stern doors enabling her to make monthly round trip voyages from Bellingham along the whole network to Dutch Harbour, a 14-day voyage of about 3,500 miles.

Across the system, sailing patterns are erratic although in recent years more regular sailing patterns have been introduced. The fleet is adjusted to match seasonal demands with many units either undergoing deep overhaul or laid-up during winter months. Maintenance is an issue with such an aging fleet and extensive work has been done on the mainliners to keep them serviceable. In late 2013 the *Columbia* was re-engined and recent fire in an electrical chamber on the *Matanuska* highlighted her vulnerability; yet until recently state funds have not been available for fleet replacement. With four main units now aged 50 or older, they simply cannot go on and work is in hand to urgently finalise and construct two new Alaska Class 'day-boats to add capacity on the scenic and much travelled Juneau to Skagway, Lynn Channel run. These in turn will allow the *Taku*, still in her original 1962 configuration, to retire and release the *Malaspina* for longer runs.

Further significant investment in fleet renewal will be required if AMHS is to avoid repeating *Tustumena's* catastrophe in 2013: on entering a four month mechanical overhaul in November 2012, serious corrosion and hull thinning was detected, requiring

complex and time consuming repairs that seem to exceed capabilities at her dry dock. Repairs, re-repairs and yet further repairs insisted upon by marine inspectors kept her out of service for almost a whole year with colossal service disruption and economic consequences.

Sailing on AMHS is a unique experience as unlike the luxury facilities, wonderful food, regular timetabling and short sectors on Norway's Hurtigruten, the Alaskan ships offer very little except basic food and berths on the longer runs, lounges, usually a small gift shop and plenty of sight-seeing. As its name implies, the system is a fundamentally part of the highway network and there is no intention of competing with Holland America or Princess Cruise Lines. Alcohol consumption, for example, is tightly controlled, furnishings and décor are spartan and food serveries open briefly at set hours. Ship-board life is set in routines and the experience is more akin to travelling on military vessels than one of Europe's ferries. However, staff are exceptionally friendly and helpful, the vessels and port calls fascinating and the experience should not be missed.

Current Fleet, major units

	Year	Grt	Pass	Berths
Le Conte	1974	3,124	300	0
Aurora	1977	3,128	300	0
Tustumena	1964 (1969)	4,259	174	68
Taku	1962	7,302	500	106
Malaspina	1962 (1972)	9,121	701	274
Matanauska	1963 (1978)	9,124	745	274
Kennicott	1998	12,609	748	314
Colombia	1974	13,009	971	313

Alaska Marine Highway's unique ro/ro side loading arrangement is illustrated here with the **Matanuska** attached to the link-span at Ketchikan in August 2013. Although almost 50 years old and operating in tough conditions, this photograph shows the vessel's immaculate condition and the care she receives. *(William Barham)*

The **Columbia**, flagship of the Alaska Marine Highway System, undertakes a weekly round trip from Bellingham, WA to Skagway, AK through the Inside Passage of British Columbia where she was captured from a passing BC Ferries service in August 2008. *(William Barham)*

Above & below: Captured at Auke Bay, Juneau, the **Taku** was second of the Spaulding designed 'mainliner' fleet ordered for AMHS in 1959. Whilst her two sisters have been extended and rebuilt, she retains her original configuration and still serves the south-eastern ports for which she was built. *(William Barham)*

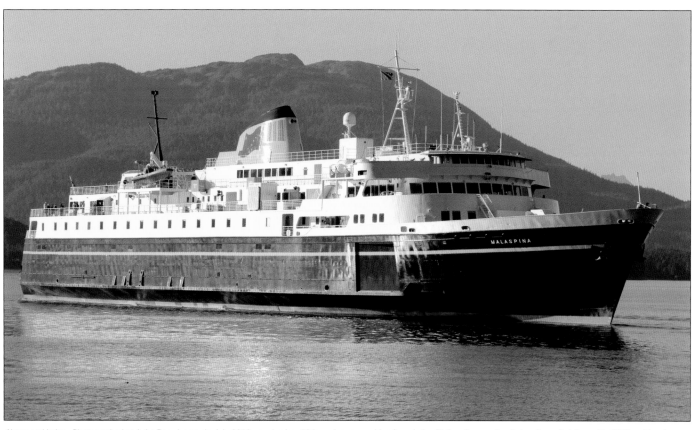

Above and below: Photographed at Auke Bay, Juneau in July 2013 carrying her 50th anniversary golden funnel, the **Malaspina** was the first major unit delivered in 1963 and has been central to celebration events in communities up and down the network fifty years on. Although lengthened by 56ft in 1972, she retains her pleasing Spaulding lines. *(William Barham)*

Newest of the major units, the **Kennicott** delivered in 1998 is captured here departing Auke Bay, Juneau in July 2013. She is equipped with a flight deck to assist with marine pollution events. *(William Barham)*

Last of the original 'mainliners' to be delivered, the **Matanuska**,1964, and similarly rebuilt to match **Malaspina**'s increased capacity in 1977. Seen arriving at Auke Bay, Juneau in July 2013. *(William Barham)*

Above and below: Built to serve daytime secondary routes in 1974, the **Le Conte** is captured here laying over at Auke Bay, Juneau between sailings. Three years later her design was used again to build near identical **Aurora**. *(William Barham)*

Above and below: At the completion of her daily service from Valdez across scenic Prince William Sound, the **Aurora** swings off her berth at Whittier in July 2013. AMHS's closest port for Anchorage, Whittier was built for military purposes during World War Two and has only recently opened up for cruise traffic. (William Barham)

Deployed exclusively on services down the Aleutian chain where ports lack any kind of vehicle loading facilities, the **Tustumena** is captured here in August 2004 at Homer swinging off her berth displaying her vehicle hoist and rear cargo door arrangements. *(William Barham)*

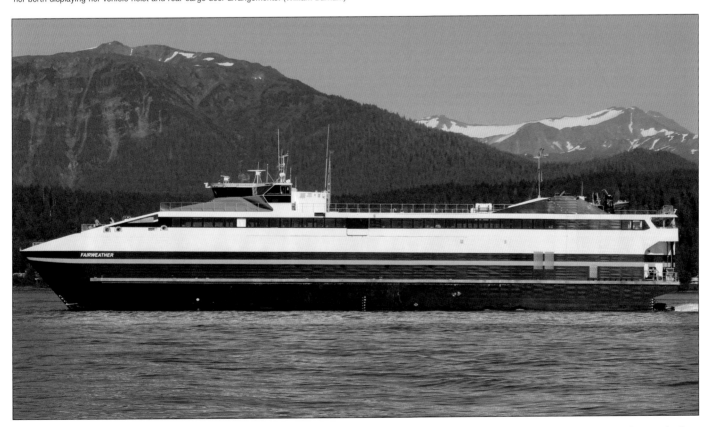

Built as one of two fast-craft to add speed and capacity on sheltered routes in 2004, the **Fairwather** streaks into Auke Bay, Juneau at the end of her 4½ hour summertime crossing from Sitka. She can accommodate 250 passengers and 35 standard vehicles. During the winter, the **Fairwather** and identical sister **Chenega** built in 2005 are laid up. *(William Barham)*

12 Fifty years on
John Hendy remembers the Isle of Thanet

Being brought up in post-war Dover, throughout the late fifties and early sixties it was initially the passenger steamer *Isle of Thanet* that captured my imagination and she became a firm favourite. Visits to Folkestone were rare but during the off-season, the veteran steamer would frequently be seen at rest in either the Granville or Wellington Docks at Dover. There it was possible to obtain a close up look at her classic lines, her Denny sheer and flair while craning one's neck to examine her slender masts and lofty buff coloured funnel.

There's no denying that by the sixties the *Isle of Thanet* looked somewhat antique, especially when compared to the latest generation of Belgian motor vessels in the Channel, but she was solid, sound and extremely well built and one couldn't fail to be impressed by her heritage. Both she and the *Canterbury* (1929) represented the golden age of cross-Channel travel before the aeroplane began to make inroads into the established trade during the 1930s and their design and execution was about as far removed from today's ferries as can be imagined.

TRENDSETTERS

The *Isle of Thanet*, and her sister *Maid of Kent* (II), were the Southern Railway Company's first contributions to the Dover and Folkestone stations following the formation of the 'Big Four' on New Year's Day 1923. In their day, both were trendsetters and represented a complete change from the earlier generations of turbine steamers. This was seen not only in their profile but also in their accommodation which was completely enclosed, unlike the previous nine such vessels which had been built at Denny's Dumbarton yard for the South Eastern & Chatham Railways' Joint Managing Committee.

Following the end of the Great War, passenger numbers dramatically increased on the Short-Sea Routes and the shortcomings of the earlier steamers became all too evident. Their open promenades tended to be wet, windy and frequently cluttered with passengers' hand luggage. The early turbines were given two continuous passenger decks; firstly the Awning Deck, which had a row of cabins built along the ships' centre line and a narrow promenade space on each side. More room was available on the Boat Deck (above) but these spaces were only available for First Class passengers. Those travelling in Second Class (then in the minority) were accommodated further aft under rather less comfortable conditions.

In rough weather the Boat Deck became uncomfortably wet as did the weather side on the Awning Deck although the provision of canvas screens served to make life a little more tolerable. Most passengers were therefore driven below or on the lee Promenade Deck but it can be seen that, just as today, passenger comfort relied entirely on the weather and so a radical departure of ship arrangement involving all the public rooms was sought. Much discussion ensued between the Southern Railway's Marine Department and the designers at Denny's who looked at the provision of one very large forward observation lounge on the Awning Deck. The structural limitations of the design made this impossible and so a compromise was sought. This was rendered possible by the provision of a single funnel uptake which set free far more internal space than had otherwise been permitted.

The *Isle of Thanet* and *Maid of Kent* were built to accommodate 1,400 passengers, with as many as 1,000 in First Class, and a crew of 63. The mahogany panelled main entrance into the accommodation was via a large deck house on the Boat Deck which also housed eight private cabins in addition to two cabins-de-luxe – all en-suite.

The Awning Deck provided the greatest change in the ships' design as it was entirely enclosed. The cabins were arranged at the sides of the ship with an observation lounge at either end. Both had sliding windows although in view of possible weather conditions, those forward were smaller. The forward non-smoking lounge accommodated 122 people while the after smokers' lounge held 110. Eight First Class cabins on each side were fitted with shared en-suite facilities between pairs of cabins. The ships' offices were also on this deck: Purser, passport, telegraph, Pullman car booking office etc.

The Main Deck, below, contained the First Class Restaurant (96 seats) which was fitted out in walnut. Adjacent to this was the Smoke Room and First Class Bar that was designed in the Old English style, finished in oak and fitted with large sofas and lounge chairs. On the Lower Deck forward were saloons for both ladies and gentlemen which were both fitted with sofas and which could be converted to berths if necessary.

The plainer Second Class accommodation boasted a starboard side dining saloon on the Main Deck for 32 and saloons for ladies (opposite on the port side Main Deck) and gentlemen (aft on the Lower Deck). After the war the accommodation spaces were reallocated to reflect the increase in Second Class travel and the fewer numbers of First Class passengers being carried. The Awning Deck's after lounge was now given to Third Class passengers (as Second Class had become until being reinstated in June 1956) while on the Main Deck the former Second Class Saloon and the Second Class Ladies' Saloon were both converted into crew cabins while a new Third Class Dining Saloon was created aft on the port side. On the Lower Deck, the after Second Class Gent's Saloon became a Third Class Bar and Smoke Room in addition to a small Gentlemen's and separate Ladies Saloon, the latter in an area immediately aft of the engine room which had once housed high density cabins for stewards and firemen.

In 1925, another new feature was the adoption of a cruiser-type stern. The older counter sterns were undoubtedly more graceful but could lead to serious damage as their form made it possible for them to over-ride the quay when berthing stern first (as was the norm) at high water. In terms of safer handling when berthing at speed, the cruiser stern was a great success although the *Isle of Thanet's* stern was transitional and a development of that employed in the 1896 trio of paddle steamers *Dover, Calais* and *Lord Warden*. As there was a tendency to catch the seas when coming astern, the design was quite different to that of the

Newly arrived at Dover in July 1925, a glistening *Isle of Thanet* is seen alongside the Prince of Wales' Pier as she is prepared to enter service to Calais. *(John Hendy collection)*

The *Isle of Thanet* is seen during the early 1950s minus the cabs on her bridge wings with which she was built. *(FotoFlite)*

Seen on official trials in the Firth of Clyde, the graceful **Isle of Thanet**'s enclosed accommodation proved to be a huge improvement on her predecessors. *(AE Glen/Bruce Peter collection)*

Coming astern towards the Admiralty Pier at Dover in 1927, the **Isle of Thanet** passes the Prince of Wales' Pier. *(AE Glen/ Bruce Peter collection)*

HMHS **Isle of Thanet** pictured at Newhaven in 1940. *(John Hendy collection)*

The ship's restaurant as built. *(John Hendy collection)*

The fo'c'sle seen from the ship's monkey island in 1964. *(John Hendy)*

The ship's elegant main stairway. *(John Hendy collection)*

The **Isle of Thanet**'s early cruiser-type stern was built to allow fast approaches to her berths. *(John Hendy)*

High capacity seating in the ship's Smokers' Lounge. *(John Hendy collection)*

In the post-war period, Folkestone became the ship's home from home when she became the Boulogne route's principal excursion vessel. *(John Hendy collection)*

Towed by the Hull tug **Headman**, the **Isle of Thanet** leaves Dover for the breaker's yard at Blyth on 10th June 1964. *(John Hendy collection)*

NEW CROSS-CHANNEL STEAMERS "ISLE OF THANET" AND "MAID OF KENT."

Built and Engined by William Denny & Bros. Ltd., Dumbarton, for the Southern Railway Company's Short Sea Route to the Continent, via Calais or Boulogne.

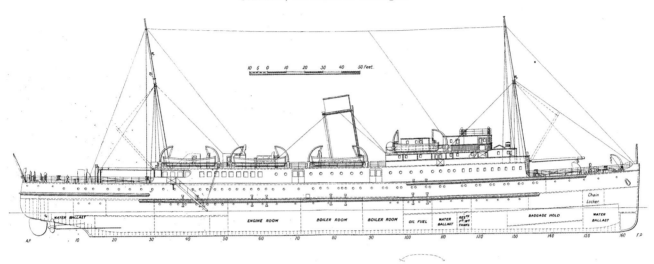

Canterbury which followed her from Denny's just four years later. On the mechanical side, the two new sisters were fitted with a twin set of Parsons' single-reduction geared turbines which were designed to run at 270 rpm at full speed. Steam was generated by five Babcock & Wilcox water-tube boilers working

The ship's wheel, engine room telegraphs and binnacle. *(John Hendy collection)*

at a pressure of 200 lb. per square inch and they were the first in the Dover Strait to be fitted with oil-fired boilers.

The *Isle of Thanet* was launched at the Leven Shipyard at Dumbarton on 23rd April 1925 and during her speed trials on 7th July, she clocked 22.25 knots. The 2,664 gross tons ship was delivered to the Southern Railway at Southampton six days later and her arrival at Dover must have caused something of a stir amongst the local seamen and townsfolk alike who had previously seen nothing like her.

How clean, elegant and so modern she looked as she lay alongside the Prince of Wales' Pier prior to entering service. Her tall funnel carried the buff and black colours of the recently formed Southern Railway and on 23rd July, just three months after her launch, she sailed to Calais and Boulogne under the command of Captain George Blaxland, while the following day completed her maiden commercial voyage between Dover and Calais.

The ship proved to be an immediate success and was immensely popular with both her passengers and crew. Her sister ship, the *Maid of Kent*, was launched on 5th August, arrived at Dover on 28th October and entered service during early November; each ship cost just over £197,000 to build. When new they were each fitted with bridge cabs in order to give the Master a degree of protection when berthing the ship during inclement weather although these proved unpopular and to improve vision a flying bridge (monkey island) was later built across the wheelhouse roof which provided the preferred position when docking. The bridge cabs appear to have been removed during the late 1930s.

The *Maid of Kent's* Master was Captain Morrison, late of the *Engadine*, but whereas Blaxland and the 'Isle' took to each other like a duck to water, Morrison's association with the 'Maid' was anything but happy.

On a perfectly calm 9th March 1926 he piled her into the Southern Breakwater after having just left the Admiralty Pier and it was said locally that the ship's engines were knocked back half

Alongside at Folkestone prior to her final
crossing to Boulogne on 15th September 1963.
(John Hendy collection)

an inch by the impact. Whether or not this was the reason, following this incident the *Maid of Kent* was certainly never as fast as her sister. As for poor Captain Morrison, who had previously confided in Captain Blaxland that he did not feel confident handling his new ship, tragedy overtook him and his sad story is a good indication of the strains and stresses with which the old cross-Channel Captains had to live.

The arrival of the 'Maid' saw the *Isle of Thanet* temporarily moved across to the secondary Folkestone – Boulogne route although there was much switching between services and between the wars, the *Biarritz* and *Maid of Orleans* (I) became the regular Folkestone steamers. Captain Blaxland had left the ship in order to take command of the 'Golden Arrow' steamer *Canterbury* in 1929, and during the 1930s the 'Isle's' Master was Captain Alfred Hammond. In the summer of 1939, the steamer first saw service away from the Dover Strait when she provided extra capacity on the popular Southampton - St Malo link.

WAR SERVICE

Just after the outbreak of war in September 1939, both sisters became hospital ships and on 21st May of the following year, whilst under the command of Captain Leonard Addenbrooke, the *Maid of Kent* met her end whilst alongside in the inner harbour at Dieppe. Both she and the Newhaven steamer *Brighton* (V) were trapped due to problems with the lock gates and footbridge which, it was suggested, had been sabotaged. There had already been air raids and the Masters of both ships were anxious move them out into the tidal harbour in order to sail back to England at a moment's notice. Without any prior warning, an air raid at 17.00 saw a stick of five bombs hit the 'Maid', two passing through the engine room skylight, two landing on the after deck while the fifth landed between the ship and the quay. The resulting explosions blew in her port side, collapsed her main mast, burst a boiler and left the ship a crippled wreck. Within three or four minutes she was ablaze and consumed by fire; 17 men were killed. Still trapped behind the lock gate, the *Brighton* was also lost through enemy bombing on the following day. It is of interest that the *Maid of Kent's* Chief Officer at the time of her loss was Mr Malcolm Brown who in 1959 became the Senior Master of the new car ferry *Maid of Kent* (III).

The *Isle of Thanet* meanwhile was distinguishing herself in the Dunkirk evacuation until her role in Operation Dynamo was cut short after being involved in a collision at full speed off Dover in the early hours of 28th May. Damage was such that she took no further part in the heroic rescue of the British Expeditionary Force but was sent to Southampton via Newhaven for repairs. The ship that had inadvertently crossed her bows was the examination vessel *Ocean Reward,* which was lost along with 13 Royal Navy personnel.

After repairs, the 'Isle' sailed to Preston where she became a Fleet Air Arm target ship until, in April 1943, she was relocated to Methil in Fife. Here she provided a sea going examination for RAF navigators and observers. In June, the ship returned south where she was fitted out as an LSI (Landing Ship Infantry) and the preparations for D Day began. Here she distinguished herself by becoming the Headquarters Ship for Force J at Gold beach.

After it was all over and with the Allied Forces advancing into Europe, the steamer became a refugee ship running between Southampton and Ostend. In 1945 she was finally returned to the Southern Railway and operated on the Newhaven – Dieppe route until the close of the following year. When the 'Isle' finally returned to the Dover Strait, it was Folkestone which was to become her home from home for the remainder of her career.

In June 1947, the *Isle of Thanet* began her long association with the seasonal Folkestone – Boulogne route whilst also enjoying occasional winter sorties on the Folkestone – Calais and the Dover – Calais 'Golden Arrow' services.

FINALE

And so she continued on her seasonal ploddings to Boulogne, also assisting on the Friday night Southampton – Guernsey service in 1949 and between the summers of 1952 and 1958. The reintroduction of weekday no-passport trips in June 1955 saw the 'Isle' become the Boulogne route's principal excursion vessel and on Wednesdays during the peak season, she was rostered purely as a day-trip vessel leaving Folkestone at 10.30 and returning from Boulogne at 18.00 with a special reduced fare of 25 shillings (£1.25). So popular did these excursions become that by the early 1960s, some 80,000 passengers a year took advantage of them.

The end came 50 years ago when on Sunday 15th September 1963 the *Isle of Thanet* set out on her very last crossing of the Channel thereby completing a glorious 38-year period of service.

The Southern Region of British Railways made much of the occasion, dressed the 'Isle' overall and invited friends and press along to see the gallant old ship into retirement.

The ship's final Master was Captain Elgar Blaxland, whose Uncle George had taken the ship on her maiden voyage back in 1925. The writer and humourist Michael Barsley penned a special piece of doggerel for the Captain on the reverse of his lunch menu which began, "Farewell Thanet, Farewell Isle, I've known you for a long, long while …" and which included the lines, "you are part of all our lives, (no matter what we tell our wives) …" which perhaps summed up the way in which so many people felt about the *Isle of Thanet*. To the sound and sight of whistles, sirens, cheers, much waving and even a few tears, the *Isle of Thanet* pulled away from Boulogne's Quai Chanzy for the final time before making fast at Folkestone some 90 minutes later. It was then to lay-up in the Wellington Dock at Dover where the vessel was offered for sale. There I visited her on a number of occasions and was able to crawl all over her from the depths of her engine room to the heights of the monkey island. The ship was 'dead' with no generators providing lighting and so these occasions proved to be something of an eerie experience. Oh how I needed a good camera!

On 10th June 1964, the rusted 'Isle' was towed by the Hull tug *Headman* for breaking up at Blyth (Northumberland) and, still a schoolboy, I had to ask my Headmaster for time off in order to witness the occasion. Thankfully, permission was granted but before the *Isle of Thanet* left the harbour, the Duke of Edinburgh's 21 gun birthday salute was fired from up on the ramparts of Dover Castle. Somehow it seemed a fitting end and many local people who witnessed her passing may have thought that behind that salute, there was a second, more meaningful, tribute.

On a personal note, late the following year I published my first ship history commemorating the *Isle of Thanet*. I seem to remember that 300 were printed and sold for 2/- (10 pence) a copy. Almost half a century later, it seems an embarrassingly feeble effort but it was the start of something which ever since has given me tremendous pleasure and has played a major part in my life.

Other books from Ferry Publications

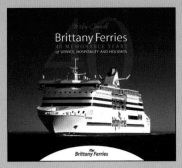

Brittany Ferries - 40 Memorable Years

Had you seen a vessel of Brittany Ferries heading across the Channel from France in 1973 it would not only have been carrying ferry passengers but fresh produce, grown by Breton farmers and on its way to the daily markets of south-west England. From this unlikely enterprise has flourished one of Europes most successful shipping companies. Today, Brittany Ferries is not only the leading ferry operator on the Western Channel. Superbly illustrates the whole fascinating story. Price £17.50 plus p&p.

Irish Ferries

In 1973, a newcomer to the Irish ferry scene began sailings between Rosslare and Le Havre. This company would grow from a single ship operator to become Irish Ferries. Today the company is market leader on the Irish Sea to the UK and France. Book also covers the history of B+I until its merger with Irish Ferries. 144 pages with over 150 pictures. A4 Style. Price £19.75 plus p&p.

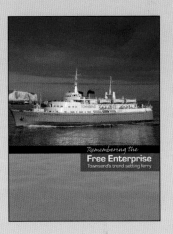

Remembering Townsend's Free Enterprise

The twin-screw motor vessel **Free Enterprise** was a ship ahead her time having been built with a stern door high enough to accommodate lorries on her after vehicle deck. When she entered service on the Dover – Calais route in April 1962, she was shockingly different with her pale green hull, wide beam and compact lines but her young architect, James Ayres, was to lead the roll on-roll off shipping revolution with a series of new and innovative designs. Price £7.95 plus p&p. **Limited print run of 300 copies.**

Order online from
www.ferrypubs.co.uk
By telephone on
+44 (0)1624 898446
By post from
PO Box 33, Ramsey, Isle of Man IM99 4LP
Please telephone or email for current postage costs.

Stena Line - Celebrating 50 Years of Service

This book brings together a selection of outstanding photographs of Stena Line's operations of both the Baltic North Sea and the UK. Compiled by Bruce Peter with complimenting text out lining the companies history and operations. Over 200 photographs in both colour and black & white. Hardback, 128 pages, A4size. Price £18.95 plus p&p.

The SeaFrance Years

SeaFrance came into being on New Years Day 1996 after splitting with former partners Stena Line on the Calais Dover link. Although a late starter in the operation of vehicle ferries across the Channel, the fleet that eventually developed was a fine collection of purpose-built ships embodying the best examples of French design and technical advancement that frequently eclipsed their British contemporaries. This book traces the post-war development of French participation in the English Channel, also briefly looking at the Dieppe Newhaven and Dunkirk - Dover operations which played such an important part in cross-Channel communications. 108 pages, Price £18.00 plus p&p.

Ferries 2014

This new edition will have features on Hurtigruten 120 years of Service, The *Viking Grace* and also a review of the ferry industry in Northern Europe. It will also feature all the usual information and data on the Ferry industry of the UK and Northern Europe with photographic material to complement the statistical information. Price £18.50 plus p&p.

Silja Line
From De Samseglande to Tallink

Silja Line and Tallink are two of the world's best known ferry companies. This book gathers together for the first time in English their entire histories, from humble beginnings with small steamers to the leisure-oriented cruise ferries of today. Partial bilingual text in Finnish. 144 pages with over 150 pictures. A4 Style. Price £22.00 plus p&p. Published late December 2013.